My name is Victoria

# My
# name
# is
# Victoria

*The Extraordinary Story of One Woman's*
*Struggle to Reclaim Her True Identity*

## Victoria Donda

**TRANSLATED BY MAGDA BOGIN**

WITH A FOREWORD BY ALBERTO MANGUEL
AND AN AFTERWORD BY PABLO A. POZZI

OTHER PRESS

NEW YORK

Production Editor: *Yvonne E. Cárdenas*
Book design: *Simon M. Sullivan*
This book was set in 11.75 pt Garamond by Alpha Design & Composition
of Pittsfield, NH.

10 9 8 7 6 5 4 3 2 1

LIBRARY OF CONGRESS CATALOGING-IN-PUBLICATION DATA

Donda, Victoria.
[Mi nombre es Victoria. English]
My name is Victoria : the extraordinary story of one woman's struggle to
reclaim her true identity / by Victoria Donda ; translated by Magda Bogin ;
[foreword by Alberto Manguel ; afterword by Pablo A. Pozzi].
p. cm.
"Originally published in Spanish as Mi nombre es Victoria by Editorial
Sudamericana, S.A., 2009."
ISBN 978-1-59051-404-7 (trade pbk. original) — ISBN 978-1-59051-
405-4 (e-book) 1. Donda, Victoria. 2. Children of disappeared persons—
Argentina—Biography. I. Bogin, Magda. II. Title.
HV6322.3.A7D6613 2010
362.87—dc22
[B]
2010040657

# Contents

# Foreword

## A CHRONICLE FROM HELL

### by Alberto Manguel

### HISTORY

In the mid-1960s, hardly anyone in Argentina could have imagined that the following decade would be the bloodiest and most barbaric in the country's history. In 1966, a military coup toppled President Arturo Umberto Illia and handed full dictatorial powers to General Juan Carlos Onganía. This ultra-conservative, antiliberal military man immediately placed all public universities under government control and disbanded all labor unions. In response to these abusive measures two popular movements were born: the ERP (Ejército Revolucionario del Pueblo, or People's Revolutionary Army), which was essentially Trotskyist, and the Montoneros, who considered themselves followers of the exiled former president Juan Domingo Perón. Their actions led to Onganía's destitution and the designation of another general as head of state. In July 1973, new elections were held, as a result of which Perón, who had been living in Spain since 1955, was returned to the presidency with 60 percent of the vote. After Perón's death only a year later, his widow, María Estela Martínez de Perón, known as Isabelita, succeeded him, but she quickly became a pawn in the hands of the army. On March 24, 1976, another coup d'état brought to power a triumvirate led by General Jorge Rafael Videla, who banned political parties and unions and imposed press censorship throughout the country. On the pretext of fulfilling "permanent obligations," Videla and the members of his junta launched a campaign of repression such as the country had never seen before. Their objective was to destroy the insurrection, but their victims were not necessarily all on the left. Anyone who opposed their regime, even a friend, relative, or acquaintance of a dissident, or anyone who in any way, however slight, had annoyed a member of the military, was considered an enemy. "A terrorist," Videla declared, "is not just someone with a bomb or a gun, but any individual who spreads ideas that run counter to Western Christian civilization."

Videla's government introduced a semi-clandestine structure to enforce its will. Its war councils could impose the death penalty on anyone, for any crime. The junta set up detention centers and established special units composed of police officers and members of the three branches of the armed forces. Headed by regional commanders who obeyed only their superiors, their mission was to kidnap, torture, interrogate, and kill. This hermetically sealed organization was impervious to influence from the families of its victims and allowed the government to deny all responsibility for the abuses it committed. For almost ten years, members of the Argentine military tortured, reduced to slavery, and murdered tens of thousands of men and women of all ages and from every social background. Inside the military prisons, hundreds of babies were torn from their mothers and sold or given to sympathizers of the regime. One of those newborns was Victoria Donda.

In 1985, two years after the end of the dictatorship, a civil court sentenced Videla to life in prison; other military leaders received shorter terms. In 1990, President Carlos Menem pardoned them all, but that amnesty was overturned in 1998, when a new court sentenced Videla to ten years under house arrest for having been an accomplice in the theft of newborns. A few months before he was set free, in August 2009, a new civil court decreed that the former dictator should be tried again for the torture and murder of political prisoners in the province of Córdoba. Unfortunately, the Argentine legal system, by and large conservative and corrupt, did not issue clear, straightforward accusations with unappealable sentences that would have put a final stop to a past that was still alive. Spread out over time, the lenient and meager sentences handed down to those responsible for thousands of atrocious crimes left the Argentine people with the impression that a whole bloody decade had ended with a simple public scolding instead of with the sort of exemplary punishment that would have met the country's moral yearning and served as a warning to future governments.

No human society is exempt from injustice. Over the course of centuries, history has inured us to the idea that the suffering of others, of our neighbors, or of strangers, is necessary in order to consolidate a nation, define its borders, and crown it in glory. One need only think of the Greek attack on Troy and the Roman genocide in Carthage. Like every other country on the planet, Argentina owes its existence to unspeakable horrors that are often forgotten. Under cover of our War of Independence and our conquest of the desert, we turned our cruelty against indigenous people and slaves, establishing from the moment we founded our first cities the principles of inequality and abuse of power. It doesn't surprise us that the hero of our national epic, Martín Fierro, should be a fugitive from the law and a deserter, since in Argentina both judges and soldiers represent a long tradition of infamy. As in so many countries, dictatorial regimes have made disobedience a heroic act for which few people are prepared.

The state of terror induced by dictatorships everywhere is always, in the last instance, a situation that takes people by surprise. During the years leading up to Nazism in Germany or Fascism in Italy, hardly anyone foresaw the scope of the criminal acts those regimes would commit. Even in countries where dictators are nothing new (as in Argentina, which suffered the bloody rule of Juan Manuel de Rosas in the nineteenth century), people always have a tendency to believe, in the peaceful interim, that such abominations could never happen again "here" or "now." Despite the lessons of history, the states that consider themselves democratic (a claim almost always open to debate) expect to be immune to gross abuses of power. Yet they're invariably mistaken. No country, not even one with a solid legal system, is safe from corruption and state violence. Under the pretext of protecting its citizens, of providing better governance so as to deliver better guidance, the power of a supposedly democratic state can quietly modify a law, suspend a right, institute censorship, and adopt repressive measures that will slowly but surely replace constitutional rules with a dictatorial regime. No country ever enjoys a true guarantee of safety. Every morning we run the risk of having our rights stolen in the afternoon, and every afternoon we risk losing them by the next morning. This is why the first obligation of every citizen is to stay vigilant and to reject any governmental transgression or abuse of power. And of course, we have a duty to bear witness.

The horrors of history, in Argentina and elsewhere in the world, must be told so that they don't remain unpunished. Otherwise, despite our pursuit of the truth, words will belong only to the guilty, who may confess and accuse themselves, but will never explain their reasons. How to explain voluntary acts of violence, the desire to make another person suffer, the ability to take pleasure from the suffering of someone else? The executioner must yield his right to speak in favor of his victim, who is the only one entitled to tell what happened.

## BEARING WITNESS

In *The Divine Comedy,* Dante imagined a hell of exemplary punishments. He began his epic poem by dividing the horrifying underground kingdom according to the seven capital sins, but soon traded that idea for a different structure, one broader and vaster, presumably closer to the geographic map of hell. Perhaps he felt that the traditional classification was too mechanical; at any rate he seems to have understood that human infamy cannot be neatly cordoned off into seven forms of excess. Dante created for us (and traversed) a hell that begins with the benign sin of indecision and the incomprehensible lack of divine grace, and ends with the deliberate betrayal of everything that makes us human. As he makes his uneasy descent, accompanied by Virgil's classic reason, Dante observes the forms of penitence and interrogates the damned. As horrific as he finds the tortures decreed by God, the confessions of those in torment are no less terrible, since they describe not the reasons for their actions, but the acts themselves.

How to account for such a failing? It is as if the souls of the damned, even after the death of the body, cannot find words for the terrible violations they have committed. Rather than a failure on Dante's part, this lack of explanation for their crimes can be attributed to an intrinsic flaw of language itself. One can recount a heinous act in all its gory details, one can describe the monstrous punishment with which such a crime is sanctioned, but to say how and why one perpetrated such a transgression seems impossible. If we find in Homer, Shakespeare, and also in the so-called erotic writings of the Marquis de Sade a certain pornography of violence, this is because such scenes have literary and philosophical justification. But there is no vocabulary for depicting the anatomy of such acts in the first person. Those who have committed terrible deeds may go so far as to say "I did that," which is already a lot, but never "I did it for this or that reason, or because I was thinking such and such."

On April 24, 1995, Víctor Armando Ibánez, a sergeant who had worked in the military jail El Campito, in Buenos Aires, confessed to the Argentine daily *La Prensa* that between two thousand and twenty-three hundred prisoners—men, women, and children—had been "executed" between 1976 and 1978. They were injected with Sodium Pentothal, a powerful drug that provokes a sort of cardiac arrest, although it induces unconsciousness, not death. Technically there is a difference between unconsciousness and coma; these victims were not in a coma, just "asleep," like anyone under anesthesia. Once anesthetized, the prisoners were thrown from unlicensed planes flying at low altitudes above the sea. Ibánez went on to say that they sometimes spotted fish the size of sharks following the planes. The pilots said that these fish fed on human flesh. A few weeks later, when Adolfo Francisco Scilingo, a navy ex-colonel, told the same story as Ibánez, President Carlos Menem called him a "criminal," claimed that he had been involved in the theft of automobiles, declared that the word of a criminal is worthless, and ordered him stripped of his rank. Ibánez and Scilingo were capable of describing these abominable acts, but neither man was up to the task of explaining why he had committed them.

In a short story based on the life of Elizabeth Báthory, who amused herself by torturing young girls to death in her chateau, the Argentine poet Alejandra Pizarnik explored the thoughts of the countess as she removed her blood-stained dress in her room after returning from the torture chamber. Pizarnik's questions still echo in our consciousness: What do torturers imagine when they finish their work for the day and go home to embrace their children, climb into bed, and wake up the next morning? Do they think back over what they did during the day, relive their actions, take pleasure in them, judge them? Presumably, if the answer is yes, they do so through instantaneous images, physical sensations, and memories, for there are no words to express the feelings, ideas, and reasoning that correspond to such recollections. Cruelty is mute.

Absent the testimony of torturers and murderers, Victoria Donda's story—courageous, responsible, honest, piercing, and illuminating—is essential reading. Collective memory is always poor: we rely on monuments and history books to remind us of the fundamental events, whether positive or horrifying, that define our national story. But stones and dates are not enough. We need the personal testimony and narratives of those who played a direct role, whether voluntarily or against their will; we need those who experienced hell and survived it to tell us the story that is part of our shared experience, the painful facts that continue to haunt our nightmares. It is essential for the victims to tell us what happened so we can admit and condemn it, and above all so we can make sure it never happens again.

# Author's Note

I should clarify to the reader that Argentina is a country where, after thirty-five years, we have just recently been able to start trying those responsible for State-sanctioned terrorism and hold them legally accountable. Until 2003, the official authorities who were accessory to the dictatorship's actions were able to achieve a legal standard that legitimized a system of impunity. This is why we have just scratched the surface: there is so much more beyond the evidence obtained and the testimonies given by the survivors and the families of the victims. Even so, guilty verdicts have not been returned in most court cases.

I have no doubts about the events I relate in the following account. The accusations I make of crimes committed by my uncle and others are based upon testimonies of people who I believe are reliable (my uncle has denied the charges). It's just that justice is yet to be served in Argentina.

I want to thank all the men and women who, courageously and despite so many years of lack of accountability, have never stopped fighting against this injustice.

My name is Victoria

# Introduction

All my life I was called Analía, the name that appears on my national identity card and birth certificate. It's also what I was called by my friends and family. I spent my childhood and adolescence in the southern suburbs of Buenos Aires, in the heart of a typical middle-class family. I attended parochial elementary and high schools, where I acquired a sense of solidarity and suffered all the rigidities of a Catholic education.

From my earliest years, I've had a rebellious, contentious nature that was diametrically opposed to that of the man and woman who raised me, whom I believed to be my parents: Raúl, a strict, reserved man who became a greengrocer after retiring from the coast guard, and Graciela, a quiet, submissive housewife.

My need to understand things and to question everything around me, along with my desire to take specific action against social injustice in Argentina, led me to become a political activist when I entered university. As I continued to oppose the right-wing discourse of my family, an ideological rift opened up between us that grew even wider as my political commitment became an essential part of me.

Contrary to what I had always believed, the differences that pitted me against Raúl and Graciela were not due only to my rebellious attitude, but had their roots in a story that went back more than thirty years. This was a story larger than my own life and those of my parents—and which embraced the history of Argentina itself during one of its blackest periods.

The last military dictatorship in Argentina began on March 24, 1976. It was not the first time the country had known this kind of regime; democratic governments were the exception rather than the rule at the time in Latin America. But this coup d'état unleashed an unprecedented, systematic wave of violence, a plan of extermination known as the Process of National Reorganization. It took the lives of some thirty thousand people, mostly young, whom the military junta deemed subversive.

The army set up virtual concentration camps throughout the country. Prisoners were tortured and then used as a source of free labor until they were found to be of no further use, at which point they were eliminated. The kidnappings and detention centers were all clandestine, which meant that victims' families had no idea where they were being held and never learned their tragic fate. This is why in Argentina no one speaks of the dead, but of the disappeared. Among the thirty thousand people who were kidnapped, tortured, and eventually killed, there were a certain number of pregnant women, who were forced to give birth under appalling conditions. Their babies were taken from them soon after they were born and given under false identities to military families or sympathizers of the junta. Once the young mothers had been "disappeared," the army believed that these children born in captivity would lead "normal" lives, forever cut off from their origins and their birth families, who continued to look for them. But they were wrong.

I was twenty-seven years old when the Grandmothers of the Plaza de Mayo finally tracked me down and informed me of my true identity, thanks to an anonymous tip from a woman who remembered seeing a soldier hand over a baby with blue thread sewn through her earlobes.

According to the testimony of certain survivors, I was born between July and September 1977. In a desperate attempt to make sure I would be recognized, my mother used a sewing needle to pierce my ears with the blue surgical thread she had been given in case she experienced complications during labor. Fifteen days later, I was taken from her arms. She never saw me again. She was subjected to one of the infamous "transfers," in which prisoners were injected with Sodium Pentothal, a powerful form of anesthesia, before being loaded onto military planes and thrown into the sea alive. Along with his colleagues at the ESMA (the Superior School of Naval Mechanics), which had been transformed into one of the most sinister torture centers in the heart of Buenos Aires, my own biological uncle had approved her "transfer."

I was thus raised in a brazen lie, knowing nothing of my true roots and loving the very people who benefited from the tragic fate of my real parents. Despite this, I grew up, developed my own personality, and managed to find my place in life through political activism, never once suspecting that I was following the path my biological parents had chosen long before.

But while I was growing up in ignorance of that past, my maternal grandmother refused to accept not only that she had lost her daughter but that she would never find her granddaughter. She hit a wall trying to extract information from my uncle and from official channels, so along with eleven other mothers of the disappeared whose babies had also been stolen, she decided to create the Grandmothers of the Plaza de Mayo. Together through the years of dictatorship and well into the restoration of democracy, they fought relentlessly to find the five hundred babies born in captivity or kidnapped as young children with their parents. Thanks to the Grandmothers and other human rights organizations, one hundred of these children have been able to recover their identities, names, history, and roots. But much work remains to be done.

Despite the pain I felt when I learned who I really was, I've been fortunate in ways not possible for hundreds of others who have no memory of their past. Thanks to my political activism, I've been able to piece myself together again, and this whole experience has made me stronger. After thinking for so long that my beliefs were in direct contrast to my family's, I now understand that in fact my activism was part of the work bequeathed me by my parents, whose ideals and character live on in me and through me.

Today, at thirty-three, I am the youngest member of congress in Argentine history and the first baby stolen by the military to play an official role in the political life of my country.

This book tells my story from the day I was kidnapped to the day I was elected to national office. I hope that through its pages, and thanks to the example of my life itself, it will be possible to retrace the last thirty years of Argentine history and to describe how a small group of men used the army in their attempt to rewrite that history. I also hope to show that, despite the systematic use of lies, the truth will always triumph. Above all, this book is my way of shouting loud and clear the truth that people tried to hide from me for years: my name is Victoria Donda.

# Cori and El Cabo

The first time I saw her, I thought I was looking at an ID photo, one of those official pictures that turn out horrible no matter what you do. She's staring straight into the camera with her eyes fixed on the lens and a serious expression on her face that can't quite hide a smile more mocking than happy. She has a strong jawline, dark, wavy, shoulder-length hair, and full lips. Like me.

I later learned that the picture had been taken after one of the many demonstrations she attended, when she was booked at a police station. It was the "official" photograph of the Grandmothers of the Plaza de Mayo, which identified my mother as one of the thirty thousand people who disappeared during the dictatorship. The same picture the Grandmothers had been using in their quest to locate me for almost thirty years. It was in fact the photograph that helped them find me.

Her name was María Hilda Pérez, although everybody called her Corita, or Petisa, which means short. Her friends in the movement, perhaps inspired by the fact that she was barely over five feet tall and had a healthy appetite, called her Chubby. Cori was born in Guaymallén, in the province of Mendoza, on April 24, 1951, and lived there until her family moved to Buenos Aires. She was the oldest of four siblings and, like any good firstborn, did not make things easy for her father, Armando, my grandfather, a militant member of the Communist Party who had spent time in jail under General Perón. Politics was always a topic of conversation in their home, and even as a girl, while her friends played house or planned their weddings, Cori sat in silence through the Party meetings her father held at home, listening to heated discussions on social justice or on the objective conditions for revolution.

When the family moved to Morón, in the western suburbs of Buenos Aires, her father taught boxing in a neighborhood gym while Cori attended the Colegio De La Salle, where she distinguished herself, among other reasons, for her high grades. In time, Cori began to visit her father in the gym and came to know the people who trained there. It was a modest barrio, with low houses and blocks of apartment buildings that had been built according to the social plans put forward during one of Perón's early terms. Most of her father's students were Peronists. Cori was on the threshold of adolescence, and at that point Argentina was a breeding ground for weak democratic governments whose existence was conditioned on the suppression of Peronism. These governments continually alternated with military ones, which in the purest Latin American tradition seized power whenever the country's ruling elite asked them to, something they did with alarming frequency.

From the time that Argentina introduced universal male suffrage, in 1912, it had had more military or illegitimate governments than genuine democracies. (Suffrage was extended

to women only in 1949.) Ever since the coup d'état that toppled Perón's second government in 1955, the Peronists and
their followers had been banned from taking part in elections, which effectively barred half the population, above all
the poor, from political representation. One of the immediate results of this situation was the rise of a whole generation
of youth for whom the idea of resistance to dictatorship did
not mean simply the return of a democracy presided over by
the army and constrained by the prohibition of Peronism,
but rather outright revolution, fueled by the different liberation movements of Latin America, especially the Cuban
Revolution.

Although Cori had been sitting in on the Communist
Party meetings that her father held in their house, like so
many other young people of her generation, she was fascinated by the figure of Perón, and above all by his late wife,
Evita. At the dinner table, she never missed a chance to
challenge her father's position, defending Peronism as the
movement that could finally guarantee the country's least-
privileged citizens full access to the government, and as
the culmination of a process that she and others believed
had been aborted by the intervention of the ironically self-
proclaimed "Liberating Revolution" in 1955 that ended General Perón's second presidential term. In the midst of heated
discussions during which she would accuse her father of
clinging to "obsolete" and "superannuated" ideas, her father
would jump from the dinner table in a rage, threatening to
look up her words in the dictionary and, if they turned out
to be insults, to "make her pay." Cori knew she could get

away with anything, though. She wasn't just the oldest; she was the apple of her father's eye.

As she continued her studies, Cori became more politically committed. She soon came to believe that it was pointless to keep debating ideas, and that in order to change the course of History, with a capital *H*, and the fate of Argentina as a whole, she would need to play a more active role. This is how she became involved in Villa Carlos Gardel, a slum not far from her home, where hundreds of poor families lived in tin-roofed shacks. Without access to education, they also lacked the social awareness to improve their situation. Joining the Peronist Youth, which continued to function at the student, neighborhood, and statewide levels even though it had been banned, Cori took her first real steps as a social activist, teaching neighborhood women to sew, teaching basic literacy to men and old people who didn't know how to write their names or count the meager wages they brought home, and organizing solidarity networks in the slum so that the residents could begin to defend themselves and see themselves as a single unified force.

But Cori's family was not well-off or even middle-class. Unable to devote herself full-time to her political activism, she began work as a secretary in the Strauss plastics factory, also in the western part of Buenos Aires. There, her strong personality and determination to speak her mind quickly made her a union delegate. Despite her youth and tiny stature, she made an indelible impression on her coworkers until the owners of the factory fired her for being too "political." Before she left she had, among other things, won the fight for a day care center for the mothers who worked in the factory. She even briefly used that center herself for my older sister, Eva, the first daughter she had with the man she called the love of her life: José María Donda, also known as El Cabo. My father.

It's virtually a national pastime in Argentina to avoid calling anyone by their real name and to use nicknames instead. José María Donda was the epitome of that tradition: while in the family and as a child he was always José, his fellow students at the Naval Academy called him El Cabo, and in activist circles he was known as Pato.

My father was the younger of two brothers in a family originally from Diamante, in the province of Entre Ríos, where, a little more than 130 years ago, a separate republic was declared and where, soon afterward, Justo José de Urquiza governed the country from the nearby city of Paraná, where Peronism later found a haven. My father was born in 1955, the same year as the Liberating Revolution's ousting of Perón. He was just a few months old when my grandfather Telmo, who worked for the Ministry of Human Development and was a union delegate, left to seek a better life for himself in Buenos Aires. There were ten years between my father and his older brother, Adolfo, which resulted in an almost paternal relationship developing over the years. It was a relationship that each of them would later interpret differently.

While in Diamante, my grandmother Cuqui had caused a scandal as a young woman who enjoyed wearing bright-colored shifts and who displayed an attitude that was too "modern" for people in such a rural backwater. When Telmo was finally settled in Buenos Aires, he brought Cuqui and their two sons to the city. Adolfo was the first to enroll in the Naval Academy. Both brothers had always been fascinated by the navy, so it seemed a natural path for them to follow, especially considering the fatherly influence Adolfo had over his younger brother. But things began to get complicated when José entered the academy. Suddenly, the boy his fellow students had immediately nicknamed El Cabo (the Captain)—in part because of his serious appearance and terse silences, but also perhaps because of his lifelong habit of cupping a cigarette with his hand to hide the light as if he were already a soldier in the trenches—would turn away from the "natural" destiny his family expected of him.

The Naval Academy was not immune to the rumblings of change that were sweeping Argentina. By the time José was in his first year of studies and Adolfo was taking the first steps of his military career, Julio César Urien, an upperclassman with strong Peronist ideas, had begun to organize for the Peronist Youth in that inhospitable setting. Not long after, on November 17, 1972, on assignment at the ESMA, Urien and a handful of other young Peronist marines decided to seize control of the school in order, on the one hand, to make sure that there would be no military resistance to Perón and, on the other, to show their opposition to the navy's latest training and organization, which, in embryonic form, was the precursor of the notorious Operations Groups, also known as *patotas* or "death squads" by those who would come to know their work firsthand. Urien and the other marines who participated in that takeover were expelled from the force, and Urien would spend the years of the dictatorship as a prisoner of the National Executive Branch, a euphemism used under the junta to describe the lucky few who, without following a particular logic, were "whitewashed" by the military government as political prisoners and sent to regular jails instead of concentration camps. It goes without saying that this classification did not spare them from torture, nor prevent them, on occasion, from turning up dead due to a supposed "escape attempt."

The chaotic sequence of events sweeping the country was the main catalyst for José's new consciousness that departed radically from family tradition. As the dictatorship that had begun under General Juan Carlos Onganía in 1966 grew weaker both economically and politically, with union and student uprisings such as the "Cordobazo" and the "Noche de los bastones largos" (Night of the Long Sticks), José definitively embraced Peronism, which at the time, especially among the youth, was a synonym of revolution. Along with a group of *compañeros* from his school, he helped to found the Union of Secondary Students (UES, precursor of the Union of University Students), which brought together the Peronist organizations of all the high schools in Buenos Aires. At first, my father joined the Revolutionary Armed Forces (FAR). The FAR exemplified the tendency of the revolutionary left to ally itself with Peronism. Although they were initially defined as followers of Che Guevara or Marxist-Leninists, their armed resistance to General Onganía's dictatorship and the brutal attack on them in 1972 (the so-called Trelew massacre) eventually brought them closer to the armed branch of the Peronist Youth, known as the Montoneros, with whom they merged formally in 1973, adopting their name.

Throughout the 1970s, the relationship between my father and his older brother grew increasingly tense, and family meals at their house in Ciudadela, on the outskirts of Buenos Aires, often led to violent political arguments that reduced my father to tears. He simply couldn't sustain the same level of aggression as his brother, who treated him like a rebellious adolescent son. On these occasions, my grandmother Coqui did her best to console her younger son, sensing how impotent he felt when confronted by his brother's personality. Perhaps Adolfo was embarrassed when his "lefty" brother opted after graduation to join the coast guard, which was considered a less demanding path for those not cut out for the rigors of a military career.

Increasingly political, José María became known as a troublemaker at the Naval Academy. The straw that broke the camel's back was the so-called sandwich strike that my father and several of his classmates organized. Halfway through each afternoon, the students received a sandwich from the institution. Sick and tired of eating the same bologna sandwich day after day, the rebels organized a strike to demand greater variety in their snacks, which put them in direct confrontation with the school authorities. My father was rewarded with a punishment designed to make him an example: a group of anti-Peronist students attacked him in their barracks one night and beat him savagely. Even though the whole episode was reported to the school authorities, the outcome of their internal investigation was that my father's entire class did not receive diplomas. Theirs was the only year in the history of the academy that no graduation ceremony was held.

It was a time of powerful political commitment with no concessions. It wasn't enough to take a position or spend a few hours a day in political activities. José María lived and breathed politics, talking and arguing with whoever was willing, and supporting his convictions with every single one of his daily actions. In a setting as strict and rigid as the Naval Academy, José María flaunted his copy of Juan José Hernández Arregui's *Peronism and Socialism*, a book banned at the time. Those who have talked to me about my father, the few who dare to joke about him while speaking of the man and not what he represents, say he probably hadn't read it; it was more like a flag, a way of reaffirming his identity as a Peronist and revolutionary in the midst of those who, twenty years before, had defeated Perón. My father and his generation at the Naval Academy were known as Class 22, and their memory lives on at the school, among both people who knew them and others who have only heard of them.

Today, many of those who took part in that innocent strike are among the disappeared. Only one of the founders of the Union of Secondary Students is still alive. My father was not so lucky.

His activism at that time was not limited to the Naval Academy and the UES; he and a group of *compañeros* also fought to reclaim public spaces, working, for example, to repair the Republic of Children, an amusement park that had been built near La Plata during Perón's second term. The political struggle was growing more radical, and there was constant debate within each group. José María belonged to the hard line, which was defeated within the UES by those who advocated a more straightforward political course. In 1972, by that point fully integrated into the military structure of the Montoneros, my father was asked to undertake "territorial" missions in the slums of western Buenos Aires province, such as Villa Carlos Gardel. Although my mother was doing similar work in the same part of the city at the same time, that was not where my parents met. It was at the University of Buenos Aires, where José María had begun to study sociology and Cori was enrolled in law school. Both subjects were taught on the campus of the law school, on Avenida Figueroa Alcorta.

I'll never really know how they met, nor under what circumstances. What I do know is that for my mother, like everything else that mattered to her, their relationship was intense and possessive. This young, awkward, tall, thin activist so slow that he was called El Pato (The Duck)—because his comrades could not accept that he didn't even know how to ride a bike—was close to a hero in her eyes, an Adonis whose magnetism was irresistible to everyone, including men.

They were the odd couple: short, passionate, plump Cori, and tall, awkward, slow Pato. My mother thought my father was the most handsome man in the world, and she could not shake off the idea that sooner or later all the women in the world would be trying to steal him away from her. My father was rather submissive toward her, and his mind was clearly on other things, so he stoically put up with Cori's jousts, no doubt proud at the same time of being loved that unconditionally. Her jealousy knew no bounds. La Negrita, an activist *compañera* whose partner had been kidnapped by the Triple A (the paramilitary Argentine Anticommunist Alliance), had to hide in Cori's house for a while. She was so nervous and desperate that she had developed an ulcer, but my mother, who could see in her only a woman trying to steal her boyfriend, kept adding spice to her meals, and the poor girl couldn't understand why her ulcer went from bad to worse.

But for my father, Cori and her family represented freedom and relaxation. This was a family with whom he could take his shirt off as soon as he walked in the door and feel at ease. In his own home, where his father's Peronism was trumped by his brother's conservative vision of the middle classes, and arguments were growing more frequent, he felt out of place and permanently tense.

The year 1973 was one of change and optimism: the dictatorship finally gave way, and elections were held. Héctor Cámpora became president on the Peronist left-wing ticket, and Perón himself returned to join the government for a third time twenty years after his defeat and exile to Spain. But it was also the year of the Ezeiza airport massacre, when groups loyal to Perón fought pitched battles over which ideology—the left or the right—should bear his name. Cori and El Pato had marched together full of hope, but they returned from the airport bearing bruises and doubts. That was also the year of their marriage. Only then did Cori's father, Armando, learn that the groom was three years younger than the bride, and because he was under twenty-one he had to obtain a special permit signed by his father allowing him to marry. Despite the two brothers being clearly opposed on political grounds, and despite their difference in age, which limited their ability to communicate with one another, Adolfo Donda was the godfather for my parents' wedding. A mere four years later, he would be a high-placed officer in the clandestine jail where my mother—his sister-in-law—would be tortured and murdered.

The political situation in Argentina was becoming more and more of a staging ground for open conflict between left and right, even within Peronism. With José López Rega and his right-wing terrorist group the Triple A, not to mention Perón himself, firmly established on a path diametrically opposed to the Montoneros, the guerrilla organization decided to go underground. This meant a definitive change in the lives of my parents and thousands of other young and not so young people throughout Argentina.

The atmosphere grew even more strained the following year, at the May Day demonstration in front of the seat of government, when Perón accused the Montoneros of being "stupid and immature." When the Montoneros responded by withdrawing from the historic Plaza de Mayo, the huge square lost an impressive third of the assembled crowd. Just two months later, Perón himself would be dead, paving the way for a witch hunt within the ranks of his party, which expelled the very youth who, two years earlier, had been defined as the "fourth leg" of Peronism.

By the beginning of 1976, the government of Isabel Perón had already asked the armed forces to take on the task of repressing the guerrilla movements, and it was impossible to halt the escalating violence of the encroaching dictatorship. By then Cori and El Pato had become accustomed to living with their blinds drawn; still, nothing could prevent my mother from expressing her delight when, thanks to some savings and the severance pay she had received when she was laid off by the Strauss factory, they were able to purchase a house of their own in the same general area of the city, close to the neighborhood of Villa Carlos Gardel.

In that house my parents raised my older sister, whom they named Eva in honor of Evita Perón, toasting the socialist world in which she would grow up. Nothing could undermine their confidence that they would be victorious and that history was on their side. Happy and proud, they sang her to sleep with the revolutionary "Hymn to the Workers":

| | |
|---|---|
| *Nuestro pavés no pasarás,* | Hey, hey, step back, |
| *Atrás, atrás, chancho burgués!* | The bourgeoisie's not coming back! |

At the time they were participating in commando operations such as the kidnapping and execution of an obscure police bureaucrat they called "Sombrerito," because of the German army beret he liked to wear when he made his rounds extorting money and intimidating the residents of Villa Carlos Gardel. But there were elements of tragicomedy too, like the time Cori's father forced her to remove a huge duffle bag full of weapons she had hidden at her parents' house. Her sisters saw her on the street in a fury, trying to drag the bag, which was almost bigger than she was, and certainly heavier. "Cowards!" she shouted at them.

Almost imperceptibly, the situation grew more hostile: they were living underground, sharing the house with other comrades. Pato, who held a key position within the Montoneros, seemed more serious than usual when he spoke of the number of *compañeros* who had "fallen," and how quickly it had happened. To make matters worse, my mother had gotten pregnant again. With me. All they could do was leave Eva with Cori's mother, expecting to take her back once things calmed down. It was 1977, the dictatorship was about to enter its second year, and stories of torture and death were accumulating by the day.

Pochi, their neighbor, says that on the day Cori disappeared in March 1977, my mother stopped by her house to share a drink of maté on her way to an "appointment." She was less bubbly and upbeat than normal, and Pochi could tell from her expression that she was anxious. When they said good-bye, Pochi sensed that something bad was going on. A few hours later, her suspicions were confirmed when my father arrived at her door, worried and depressed.

"Cori's been arrested," he said, without looking at her. "I came to say good-bye."

"Wait a minute. What do you mean? What happened? Where are you going?"

"My brother set her up. They were waiting for her at the station at Morón, where she had agreed to meet someone. I can't stay here anymore."

The same brother who had protected him his whole life, the brother who had been the witness at his wedding, and who had even offered them an opportunity to leave the country, had finally given in to everything that stood between them. He had followed orders and handed over the key to capturing my father: his sister-in-law.

That afternoon in the middle of March the heat was unbearable in the area around the train station of Morón. My mother arrived a little early for her appointment, in part out of nervousness and in part to make sure there was nothing out of the ordinary in the environs. She managed to meet up with the man she was supposed to see, but before they were able to exchange a word they realized that they were surrounded, and a death squad had them in its grip. They were beaten, black sacks were thrown over their heads, and they were pushed into a pickup truck. It was a squad from the air force. They put the man in the back and my mother up front in the cabin, between the driver and a conscript. When they stopped at a red light, her *compañero* jumped off the truck and ran as fast as he could while the members of the squad chased after him. The driver and the soldier also got out of the car, so my mother, pregnant as she was, seized the opportunity and ran in the opposite direction. She ran desperately, following the railroad tracks, hoping to find another station and a train waiting to help her get away. But as she ran, the heel of one of her shoes broke off. She ditched them both and ran on barefoot, in a frantic attempt to save us both, until she heard a shot ring out behind her. They had killed her friend. In no time at all they caught up with her, and this time there was no escape. The first stop in her abduction was Police Station No. 3 in Castelar, which served as a kind of holding pen for people who had been *chupados*—literally "mopped up"—by deployments of the navy in the west of Buenos Aires. There, between tortures and abuse, they held her for three months.

A few months later, my grandmother Leontina, Cori's mother, would crisscross the platforms in the Ramos Mejía station trying to fulfill her daughter's last wish: my mother had said that if anything happened to her, Leontina should look for the street musician who played there and ask him to play "her" song, a Peruvian waltz called "Hilda."

| | |
|---|---|
| *Pero al comprender que mi vida ya cambió,* | I understand now, Hilda, that my life has changed, |
| *Fuiste Hilda tú mi tentación,* | You were my temptation, |
| *Fuiste Hilda tú la que dejaste en mi ser,* | But all you left in my soul, Hilda, |
| *Honda desesperación.* | Was desperation. |

With tears in her eyes, Leontina began a tireless struggle to win back her daughter and her unborn grandchild. Not long afterward, she and eleven other women whose children and grandchildren had also been kidnapped founded the association of the Abuelas de la Plaza de Mayo—the Grand-mothers of the Plaza de Mayo. In the midst of the dictator-ship, running risks she would never have dreamed of taking in her days as a modest homemaker, my grandmother Leon-tina would raise the same banner as her daughter and, in her own way, continue the struggle my mother had begun: the fight for social justice.

Much less is known about the circumstances of my father's arrest. The same day they kidnapped my mother, he showed up at Pochi's house to say good-bye. After that, he went to the place where they had "picked up" Cori. He questioned people in the neighborhood and managed to reconstruct the events leading up to the moment she was seized. Follow-ing her footsteps, he arrived at a square where he found her shoes—either tossed behind a bush or next to some tree. I don't know if he cried or shouted or was silent, but people who lived near the train station of Morón were shocked to hear the sound of gunfire in the middle of the night. It was my father, emptying his gun into the air.

From that moment on, everything I know about my par-ents and their fate is based on mere wisps of information gleaned from contradictory eyewitness reports, friends, and acquaintances. Only a handful of them survived the torture and unspeakable horrors of that secret parallel world of under-ground jails—better described as concentration camps.

After managing to lie low for a while, my father was cap-tured by the air force sometime toward the middle of May, although few details are known. Before his arrest, my grand-mother Coqui saw him only a few times. They met in secret

23

near the Basilica of Luján, and just for ten minutes. Maybe
out of desperation he contacted his brother and asked him
to try to help my mother. Maybe that's why he was caught.

According to two survivors who were held during the
same period in Police Station No. 3 and whose declarations
coincide, it's likely that Cori and El Cabo saw each other
one last time in that sinister place. Of the two of them, the
military considered my father the more valuable one, because of his position in the Montoneros and the information
they believed they could extract from him. They probably
picked up my mother as a way of getting to him, and for
having been in the wrong place at the wrong time. One
morning, they came for her and took her up to the third
floor of the station, which was where they conducted their
interrogations. But it was not to question her again; it was a
face-to-face: they wanted to put a prisoner in front of her to
clarify their suspicions regarding his identity, and they believed my mother knew him. My mother must have entered
that poorly lit room that stank of fear, and for one moment
she must have met the gaze of the man she loved more than
anybody in this world, the man she thought could have the
most beautiful women he wanted. But not a muscle moved
on her face or his. They showed no sign of recognition. They
said nothing and managed to fool their torturers, if only for
a moment. That was the last time they saw each other before
they died.

After that, they probably sent my father to a *centro clandestine de detención* (clandestine detention center), or CDD,
most likely Mansión Seré or Campo de Mayo, but there

are no witnesses or survivors to corroborate it. All that remains of him is a handwritten letter that was delivered to my mother's family, which we can't help but suspect his kidnappers forced him to write. It was given to my grandmother Coqui.

> . . . the pain of not knowing the torture to which my wife is being subjected, nor whether my child has been born or not. Both families should join forces and raise my daughter. Try to help Cori. Speak with Donda.

They did speak with Donda—my father's brother, Adolfo. Again and again, they begged him to intercede. Again and again he refused, saying he knew nothing.

Shortly after the failed face-to-face, Cori was transferred to what would be her final destination: the underground jail at the ESMA, under the direct command of the head of the navy, Emilio Massera, known as "Admiral Zero." Here such well-known characters as Jorge "the Tiger" Acosta, Alfredo Astiz, Adolfo Scilingo, Rubén Jacinto Chamorro, and, of course, the young frigate captain in charge of Operations Group 3.3.2—Adolfo Donda—plied their trade in the arts of torture, extortion, and robbery.

The ESMA was one of the most important clandestine prisons of the dictatorship. An estimated five thousand people, of whom only a handful survived, passed through its cells. Perfectly organized, like the entire system of repression the military had set up, its function was divided into different areas that were specifically designated for kidnapping and torture, for the theft and distribution of the property and possessions of the detainees, and for counterintelligence, using other captives as slave labor whenever necessary. The torture chambers of the ESMA saw such illustrious figures as Norma Arrostito, one of the first leaders of the Montoneros; the French nuns Alice Domon and Léonie Duquet; Azucena Villaflor, one of the Mothers of the Plaza de Mayo, the organization that the Grandmothers of the Plaza de Mayo branched off from; and the Montonero journalist and leader Rodolfo Walsh, who was already dead when they brought him there.

This was where they had set up the apple of the eye and the greatest pride of Rubén Chamorro: the Sardà, or maternity ward, as it was known after the clinic of the same name in Buenos Aires. Located in Section 4 of the ESMA, the Sardà was a minuscule room about six feet long by three feet across where pregnant prisoners were brought from different concentration camps in order to give birth. They would never see their babies again.

The captives lived, were tortured, and worked in the attic of the Officers' Mess, a horseshoe-shaped space with a sloping mansard roof and no windows, where dim naked bulbs hung every few feet, bathing the prisoners' haggard bodies in a yellow, cadaveresque glow. Divided into two equal groups, the prisoners slept one on top of the other in one of the two Ls, without being able to remove the black sacks that had been placed over their heads. In yet another example of the military's sense of humor and imagination, this side of the building was called "the Hood." The other side was subdivided into "the Warehouse," where booty seized from prisoners' homes was stored, and an improvised work area where certain prisoners spent their day translating the news, forging documents, or carrying out administrative tasks. Those workers were separated from one another and visible at all times through the Plexiglas divisions that had given rise to that section's name: "the Aquarium." The area above the attic, a miniature reproduction of the floor below, housed two water tanks that supplied the whole building. This was Capuchita ("Little Hood"), or the little torture chamber, where prisoners from other branches of the armed forces were brought to be tortured. The new arrivals were entitled to spend some time in the basement, where the first round of torture was conducted and where it was determined whether a prisoner could be of use and, if so, what tasks he or she would be assigned, as well as whether additional torture was required. Apparently the day she arrived at the ESMA, Cori lucked out, because Alfa, the best of the three women guards, was on duty. In ascending order of brutality, she was followed by Beta and Charlie. Since my mother was pregnant and almost full-term, they didn't take her to Capuchita but let her go up to the third-floor attic with the other prisoners. There she was allowed to enjoy her first meal: a "navy steak," a new euphemism meaning an ordinary orange.

Despite the torture, despite the months of captivity and humiliation, despite her pregnancy, and despite not having even been able to embrace her husband when they were face-to-face, my mother hadn't lost one iota of her character and strength. She refused to eat, giving her orange to the young woman lying next to her, with whom she exchanged her first few words. Perhaps because she was pregnant, or because of a perverse notion of the "favorable treatment" she might be due as the sister-in-law of Adolfo Donda, my mother was later allowed two oranges instead of one, and from time to time they let her eat twice a day.

The room that would later be called the "maternity ward" didn't exist yet at the time, so my mother was sharing the space with more than two hundred people whose faces she couldn't even see. Like everything that happened in the underground jails, how my mother spent her remaining days remains a mystery. All I have to go on are bits and pieces of stories and anecdotes, always half veiled, because it's impossible for the survivors to fully express what they went through, and because a kind of delicacy imposes itself before they convey the unspeakable to someone who's not prepared to hear it.

One day in July, August, or September 1977, in the tiny room called Sardà, my mother finally went into labor. The birth was attended by Jorge Luis Magnacco, the gynecologist of the Naval Hospital, and the midwife was Lidia, a nineteen-year-old witnessing her first childbirth. All the kidnapped mothers who went into labor at the ESMA were forced to write a letter to their families informing them of the birth and asking them to take care of the baby. It goes without saying that these letters were never delivered, just as the families never learned if a child had been born and, if so, whether it was alive. The cynicism with which the military operated was well-known to their victims, who had learned that "transfer" meant murder, "steak" meant orange, and "machine" meant electric cattle prod. This is why Cori always knew that her mother Leontina would never read her letter.

The women knew that their babies would never reach their families, but there was no way they could possibly have imagined the perfectly oiled system the military had put in place, whereby the newborns were offered to the families of military officers or those sympathetic to the junta, who were even allowed to put their names on a waiting list at the Naval Hospital. At that time, in their innocence and ignorance of the true dimensions of the situation, Lidia and Cori came up with a plan: using the needle and blue surgical thread they had been given in case of an unexpected vaginal tear, they sewed two loops through the earlobes of Cori's baby girl. Who knows—maybe they believed that the infant would end up in an orphanage like any abandoned child, and that one day in the future, once Cori was freed, they would be able to use that symbolic descriptive mark as a way to find her. Dirty, covered with wounds and scars that told the story of the preceding four months of her life, Cori did not give up her eternal confidence, her strength, and her belief that sooner or later they would eventually win, and that the military would have to leave through the same window they had broken in order to come in. She named me Victoria, and for a few days she was able to believe that her little girl was a sign of change to come.

Two weeks later, Lieutenant Héctor Febrés, better known as "Selva" ("the Jungle") because he was said to be the most animal-like of all the beasts, the man in charge of maternity at the ESMA, took Cori's baby from her side. He also took her letter.

Thanks to Dr. Magnacco, who stamped his signature onto the forged birth certificate of the child who from that day forward would be known as Analía, I was given to a couple of modest means, Graciela, a housewife, and Raúl, a coast guard lieutenant and good friend of Febrés who was making a name for himself in various tasks at the ESMA that required a "strong hand." At that moment, Analía was born and Victoria was condemned to disappear—like her mother and father, whose names belong to the innumerable lists of family and friends we can only assume are dead, but whom we are denied the right to mourn.

What was the true role played by my uncle Adolfo in the kidnapping and disappearance of his brother and sister-in-law, and in the abduction of his niece? If the whole truth ever emerges, it won't be any thanks to him. At the time of this writing, he refuses to let me visit him in his glass cell, insisting that I'm not a family member. But "Donda" was a leading force of the death squads. So on the Wednesday in 1977 when it came time to decide, as they did every week, which prisoners were going to be "transferred," he agreed to the transfer of my mother. He gave permission for her to be led down to the basement, manacled hand and foot with a hood over her head, when she could barely walk because she had so recently given birth. He allowed her to be taken to the infirmary, where Manzanita (Little Apple) or one of the other assassins injected her with a dose of Sodium Pentothol, or "pentonaval," as it was sarcastically known among the soldiers, because it was supposedly the navy's favorite form of anesthesia. And he kept her alive and conscious while the military truck, filled with sedated prisoners, rumbled toward the port, where they loaded her onto the Fokker airplane that took off that night high above La Plata River. It was there that they threw her out into the void, still alive and incapable of defending herself.

A few months later, one of the few survivors of the ESMA would have the unfortunate privilege of overhearing one of Donda's self-assured monologues, in which he congratulated himself and bragged about his ruthlessness:

"This is a war. And in a war you can't show mercy to your enemy. I didn't show mercy to my own brother, who was a Montonero. And I didn't show mercy to my sister-in-law, who was brought here to the ESMA just like you. And she was transferred, just as you'll be if you don't do what we tell you. I didn't show them the least preferential treatment and I didn't feel the slightest guilt, because this is a war, and they were on the other side. That's how it goes: either we win or you do. So you might as well cough up whatever you know . . ."

# Childhood

The southern part of metropolitan Buenos Aires, crisscrossed
by the old tracks of the General Roca Railway, extends for
dozens of miles beyond the perimeter of the capital. Like
most of the world's large metropolitan areas, it consists of
a series of concentric circles through which the suburban
middle class gradually gives way, station by station, to more
sparsely populated, poorer neighborhoods, dotted here and
there by squatter camps that seem intentionally put there to
remind us that Argentina is and will remain a country that
moves forward (or back) at two different speeds.

I spent the early part of my life, up to the age of twelve,
on the border that separates the first from the second of
these concentric social circles, between the neighborhoods
of Berazategui and Florencio Varela. It might seem like a
minor detail, but even today, after everything that's happened, whenever I think of where I spent my childhood,
memories well up in my throat. All my life I considered that
neighborhood to be the place where I was born, that family
to be my family, that chapter of my life as belonging to the
overlapping lives of so many other people. But as I write
this book, letter by letter and word by word, trying to put
what I remember of those years to paper, the word "born"
feeds on my memory like a parasite, emptying it of meaning.

Childhood seems to me the one period in life where nothing should be questioned, where one's existence is "given" through daily experiences in which everything is safe: family, friends, possessions. To describe that reality through the filter of a truth learned many years later would be neither fair nor honest, and however complicated it may seem to refer to those things as constituting an unquestionable truth, that is, in fact, the way I experienced it. Those streets of Berazategui, with their grassy pathways and the rows of plane or linden trees in whose shade the neighbors protected themselves from the intense Buenos Aires sun, are part of my life—just as Analía is part of my life. A part that, no matter how much I now know about the circumstances that placed me there, I still consider true.

As with most people, my childhood memories are fragmentary, almost like small frescoes or photographs that portray feelings more than facts, and always colored by an imagination that, when we're so young, blends with reality to create a total picture as blurry as it is definitive. This is why, despite everything, my childhood remains a period of wide-open spaces and small adventures. It is also the time in which I must have begun to forge the character that seemed to me back then so hard to account for, but which I now see reflected in the memory I've been able to recover of my mother.

I doubt anyone would have used the words "docile" or "easy" to define me. My behavior was the exact opposite. Without ever becoming unmanageable, but also without ever depriving myself of the chance to annoy those around me, I would probably have been best described as a tomboy. In most cases, a tomboy is simply understood to be a girl who refuses to be submissive, and who would rather play physical games than sit around with a bunch of other girls and a plastic tea set. I always got along better with boys, not only because I could throw myself to the ground or climb trees like one of the gang, but also because my awareness of belonging to the so-called weaker sex allowed me to lord it over my little friends as much as I wanted to. I would say that ever since I was a little girl I knew how to choose the advantages of each sex over the disadvantages, in a kind of balancing act that still works for me today. I almost never show up at a demonstration or any other political event without high heels, and the huge hoop earrings I always wear seem to be my way of remembering the little blue threads my mother used to identify me. But I'll never be the first to run if there's a conflict, and I'll always be in the front line when it comes to "giving and getting."

Those were the years when the person I now call Raúl was my *papá* and when I called his wife, Graciela, my *mamá*. Of all that, of the family I called my own for so many years, there remain feelings I can't and won't deny, feelings I have to keep to myself, because they can't be shared with anyone or even verbalized without arousing a sense that merely having them constitutes a kind of betrayal of my own convictions. Perhaps the only relationship I have preserved intact from that time, impossible to dissolve by legal means or public declarations, is the one with my younger sister, Clara. Today I know for sure that we don't share genes, blood, or family. And I also know that none of that changes my affection for her and my eternal need to protect her. Today we share a history, one that is bigger than either of us and that defines us both, along with our parents, as victims. Since my duty is still to look after her, and relying on that shared fate that unites us more than any biological tie ever could, I've decided to leave her out of this story as much as possible. Clara needs my support and understanding, as she always has. For now, the best way to support her is by excluding her from these pages. It should be up to her to decide when and how to tell her own story.

When I look back on those moments, I remember a time of plenitude. There were days spent out on the street playing *Charlie's Angels* with boys and girls in the neighborhood or weekends at my grandmother's house in Lanús, where Mario, one of my numerous childhood boyfriends, would always be waiting for me to go out for a walk. Hand in hand, we were carefree and thought of ourselves as adults.

So once again, almost like a constant in my life, Mario floats back into my mind just as so many others have disappeared into the fog of memory. But Mario was not the only one, perhaps not even the most important: my relationships with men have always mattered since I was a child, and I've never denied myself the chance to be surrounded by them. Mario shared my affection with two other special boys whose names escape me but whose faces are still vivid in my mind.

One of them was our neighbor. We lived in a middle-class neighborhood, in a small complex of five-story houses with faded yellow walls, and this particular boy won me over with an insistence and a gallantry as inappropriate in a seven-year-old kid as they are rare in grown men. Every time he came by, he brought a bouquet of flowers he had picked downstairs and wrapped in a page from his notebook, offering them to me as if to reaffirm our love. The third contender was Gustavo, or maybe Gonzalo. I'm no longer sure, even though he was the one I saw most often, because we went to the same Catholic school. In a country where public education had been largely abandoned by the state, and where the resulting decline had had a more noticeable effect in the outlying regions of the capital than within the city of Buenos Aires, for families like mine religious schools became the only affordable means to obtain an education that didn't mean mortgaging their future. At Sacred Heart, even though it was coed, the repressive side of the religious training was predominant. That may even be why I had a boyfriend in school; there are few things I remember with more pleasure about that place than the fury of the Mother Superior whenever she caught me walking hand in hand with Gustavo. Considering how I was at seven, with my head full of sins, if she knew who I was now, I'm sure all her worst suspicions about me would be confirmed: that I was destined for her personal vision of hell.

Still, it's also true that my rebelliousness and tendency to draw attention to myself didn't always produce a negative result in school. In first grade, my teacher decided to use reverse psychology with me, probably more as an act of faith on her part than anything else. She made me the student representative in all the official school events. Flag days, plays, musical productions, religious feast days—you name it, I was onstage. Since Raúl and Graciela had few reasons to be proud of my academic achievements, at least for a time they could take pride in seeing "their" daughter at the front of the auditorium.

Of course, only a little child can enjoy such happiness; I was too young to have a frame of reference that would have enabled me to understand my life through any other prism. But while Analía was peacefully ensconced with her parents and her little sister in their daily lives, in the heart of my true family a terrible catastrophe was taking shape.

According to the testimony of witnesses, Frigate Captain Adolfo Donda Tigel, alias Palito, alias Jerónimo, having participated in the kidnapping, torture, and disappearance of his own brother and sister-in-law, and having given his youngest niece to one of his collaborators, had one last mission to accomplish: he wanted my sister Eva for himself.

My uncle did very well for himself during his years as a torturer at the ESMA. From the start of the repression, he was part of the leadership of Operations Group 3.3.2, which was in charge of kidnapping targets designated by the higher-ups of the dictatorship. Later on, he was named chief of intelligence of the command, a post he shared with another well-known torturer, Miguel Angel Benazzi, alias "Manuel." The French nuns Léonie Duquet and Alice Domon, Carlos Lorkipanidse, Víctor Fatala, and many others who will never be able to testify against them passed through their hands.

In the years after my mother's kidnapping, the gulf between her family and my father's began to widen, but it split apart completely when Adolfo Donda stole my sister Eva.

Over the years, Cori's siblings had gone hundreds of times to see him, continuing to believe that if there was a man with feelings behind that cynical smile, he was the only person capable of saving his brother and their sister. Again and again he told them he knew nothing; he must have been just as convincing when he promised my mother that I would be placed with my real family. My grandmother Leontina was already involved by that point with the Grandmothers of the Plaza de Mayo. Jointly and individually, the Grandmothers had filed multiple requests for habeas corpus and other formal measures with a host of international organizations, never losing hope that they would eventually at least find their grandchildren who had been born in captivity.

One day, Adolfo Donda approached my grandmother and asked her to sign a paper acknowledging the death of her daughter Cori. Leontina refused. Until she saw her daughter's body, she said, she would never accept that she was dead. The two grandmothers, who up until that point had agreed to share custody of their granddaughter, began to drift apart due to Leontina's "political involvement." At the time, no one was yet aware of the role my uncle had played in the family's fate, although they already had their suspicions. It wasn't long before they had their first proof.

In 1987, when democracy returned to Argentina, Eva fell definitively into my uncle's hands. For several years she had been living with our paternal grandmother, Cuqui, because it was feared that Leontina was too "exposed." Alfonso "Palito" Donda had been a loyal soldier according to the expectations of the navy, and at moments like this, faithful service is repaid. So when he sued my grandmother Leontina for custody of his niece, instead of being sent to rot in jail, my uncle Palito, my mother's accused murderer, was made my sister's guardian. It is possible that some of the judges who heard the case had also kept quiet during the dictatorship. Perhaps relying on outdated expectations that had long since fallen by the wayside, the judge decreed that since the child's grandmothers were unable to agree on Eva's care, it was in the child's best interest to live with the family member next in line. As icing on the cake, Adolfo indulged himself in a final symbolic act, striking from my sister's papers the name Eva, which had meant so much to my parents, and keeping only her middle name, Daniela. Once again, lies and disappearance had the upper hand, and the truth seemed dead and buried.

By then, there was no longer any doubt about the role my uncle had played during the years of the dictatorship. Once democracy has been restored, the Center for Legal and Social Studies summoned the families of victims of the junta to consult their archives, which would eventually become the basis for one of the most important books ever published in Argentina, *Nunca más* (Never Again). This was a sourcebook made up of survivors' accounts, a handful of documents that had been uncovered, and denunciations by family members, all of which were compiled and published by the National Commission on the Disappearance of

Persons (CONADEP). Here, for the first time, Cori's family was able to see where their daughter had been taken: to the School of Naval Mechanics, the ESMA. On the list of those in charge of that torture center was the name they had come to suspect would be there: Adolfo Miguel Donda Tigel.

Did my grandparents Cuqui and Telmo know the role their older son had played in the disappearance of his younger brother? For a time, probably not—in part, strange as it may seem, because Argentina experienced the dictatorship without being fully aware of what was really going on in those concentration camps; and in part because there aren't many people in this world who would be capable of assimilating and processing the horror of having a monster as their son. Cuqui died in the mid-1980s, without ever learning what had become of her younger son and without ever daring to look his older brother in the eye. Telmo survived her by ten years, although he died before we were able to meet. Still, I'm sure he suspected Adolfo, and that his heart must have broken every time he thought about his direct involvement in my mother's death and, by extension, my own disappearance. When I later went to the human rights archives on my own, I discovered more than fifty habeas corpus motions in my grandfather's name, which he had doubtlessly made behind my uncle's back, requesting information on the whereabouts of my father. Those who were lucky enough to know him told me that once, at work, someone asked if he had children. His laconic reply barely hid the pain of an impotent father, who must have felt guilty to the end of his life. "I had two sons," he replied. "One died because he was a Montonero. The other one is dead to me, because he was a murderer."

The suffering of my paternal grandparents during all those years is mine now, and for the rest of my life I'll bear an irrational guilt for not having been able to meet them. Perhaps there is an "other side" from where they can see me now and know that I'm all right. From where they can hear me thinking of them and understand that I know them without having met them, the same as my parents, and that despite all the attempts that were made to ensure that my blood ties would be severed forever, I've been able to go back and reconstitute myself, my past, and my roots, of which they are a part.

With the advent of democracy in Argentina, the terrain was less hospitable for the leaders from the ESMA to continue enriching themselves with the possessions and property that had piled up in the Pañol, or Storeroom, the section of the Officers' Mess adjacent to the Aquarium, where they took all the "war booty" stolen from their raids on victims' houses during the kidnapping missions of the death squads. Democracy's first steps were tentative and timid, which gave the military sufficient time to erase most of their tracks, wipe the blood from the lapels of their uniforms, and tuck their electric cattle prods away to await a more propitious moment. Adolfo Donda managed to have himself posted as the naval attaché to the Argentine embassy in Brazil, with the double intent of maintaining a safe distance from the likeliest reprisals for his acts and of keeping a watchful eye on a man considered one of the main enemies of the regime: the former Montonero leader Mario Eduardo Firmenich, alias Pepe, who still considered himself the general secretary of the Montoneros. It wasn't long before a few specialized publications implicated Adolfo Donda in Firmenich's capture and eventual extradition.

There was a moment, almost too brief to be believed, when the idea of a justice as impartial as it was implacable seemed to take hold in Argentina. After the publication of *Nunca más,* and after the trials of those directly responsible for the massacre perpetrated during the eight blackest years in the history of Argentina, it now seemed time for the second tier in command, the so-called men on the ground, to have their day in court. Along with many others, my uncle was called to account by the justice system and placed in preventive detention, when he awaited the result of a trial in which he was accused of seventeen crimes of kidnapping, torture, and death. But the democratic spring was short-lived, and at Easter 1987, a military uprising led by Major Ernesto Barreiro and Lieutenant Colonel Aldo Rico succeeded in twisting the arm of the law and in forcing then president Raúl Alfonsín to approve two terrible laws that would not be nullified for another fifteen years: the Law of Due Obedience, which established distinct degrees of responsibility based on the military chain of command, and the Law of Final Stop, thanks to which all crimes not brought to justice by that point could no longer be punished. This would be the first in a series of tough blows to legitimate democracy and a clear sign that although they were no longer in power, the military still considered themselves (in a few cases correctly) the rightful owners of political power in Argentina. Thanks to the most unjust laws ever approved by the Argentine Congress, hundreds of assassins and torturers were set free. Thanks also to the new climate of tension and defeat that settled over those who had fought so hard for liberty and justice, my grandmother Leontina began to succumb to the constant threats and pressure from Adolfo Donda, who had successfully won custody of my sister Eva. My mother's disappearance had done more than just leave an empty space in the family that her supposed death would always occupy. My aunt Inés, the youngest daughter, was the first to leave, finding the situation and her impotence to do anything about it unbearable. Inés chose exile from the country that hid her own sister's fate from her, and moved to Toronto, Canada. Her brother and sister soon followed with their respective families. Weakened although not defeated, my grandmother Leontina, one of the founders of the Grandmothers of the Plaza de Mayo, who had fought tirelessly to discover the truth about her daughter and grandchild, followed her family to Canada. Palito the torturer, Palito the murderer, my uncle Palito, had won the battle. What he didn't suspect at the time was that in the end he would lose the war.

While the family I still didn't know was shaken and undermined by conflicts from within and without, my life continued on its innocent, unsuspecting path. Once, listening to a speech by Juan Cabandié, the seventy-seventh grandchild recovered by the Grandmothers of the Plaza de Mayo, I remember being particularly struck when he said that he had always felt his name was Juan, not what had been written on his forged birth certificate. He had had recurring dreams in which a woman, who must have been his mother, was giving him her breast and murmuring "Juan, Juan." As a teenager he had asked his friends to call him that. Without knowing why, without knowing anything of his true past or without so much as suspecting that, like me, he had been born in the "maternity clinic" of the ESMA, Juan always knew that the name he grew up with did not belong to him. My case is very different from his in many respects. But there are common threads. Without ever knowing why, all through my childhood I loved to pretend that I was actually a princess, the heiress to a magical distant kingdom, and that my real name was Victoria. In fact, my fixation with the name Victoria accompanied me all my life. When my best friend, Vicky Grigera, and I were law students at the University of Buenos Aires, working together on political actions, we used to talk about what we would name our children. Needless to say, my daughter was going to be Victoria.

Between going to school, playing outside with the other children in the neighborhood, and visiting the woman I still want to call my grandmother, my life as a child was not very different from that of every other little girl my age. But the moment I most looked forward to was the weekend, when I would spend the whole day with Raúl in his greengrocery, which was just outside the city limits of Buenos Aires, in

Dock Sud. Raúl had gone into this business after retiring from the navy, and for me it was like a dream to be surrounded by boxes of apples, lettuce, zucchini, and every other kind of fruit and vegetable stacked one above the other in a perfect image of domesticated nature. A delightful old Yugoslav couple lived behind the store, and I spent lots of time with them too. The man was called Iván and his wife was Eugenia, and although my memory of Iván is too blurry to portray more than his broad shoulders and a pair of hands that showed decades of hard physical labor, I remember Eugenia as clearly as if she were standing before me as I write: she was tiny, so tiny, even to a ten-year-old girl who was still under three feet tall. She was blond and struck me as very white, which I assume was due to her Slavic roots. In Argentina, as in so many other countries, the chromatic ascent of skin color goes hand in hand with social status. Dark is poor, which is probably why I was surprised to find someone so white living in a precarious shack barely held together by old planks and scraps of sheet metal. Eugenia was also quite fat, and her hair was very, very short. She always wore loose, threadbare shirts that hid the contours of her body, and I never met anyone who sweated the way she did. It made no difference whether we were in the midst of one of those humid, torrid summers when the air is thick enough to chew or in one of our Buenos Aires winters where the sun and rain take turns throughout the day without raising the temperature by even one degree: Eugenia sweated. The sweat stains would spread below her armpits and circle around her immense breasts and bulging stomach, and her forehead and upper lip would fill with little beads of water, as if she were weeping from every pore of her body.

I spent whole afternoons with her and Iván, playing in the courtyard where there were still a few stray patches of grass or pretending to be a schoolteacher, trying to teach my two old friends their ABCs. In exchange, I acquired, especially from Iván, my appreciation for radishes. Like most children my age, I had definite ideas about what I liked and what I didn't. Radishes belonged to the group "I hate them," but when Iván dug between the weeds, pulled out one of those rosy little spheres, wiped it clean, and placed it in my mouth with a gesture of delight, I found it irresistible. Ever since then, whenever I spot a radish, I see that curious couple and taste again the wonderful flavor I experienced when I realized that, for once, I didn't know everything.

My relationship with Iván and Eugenia came to an abrupt end because of my eternal need to rebel and to do exactly the opposite of what I was asked. I was always unable to digest bananas and had been given strict orders not to eat them. That was enough for me to decide one day to steal a huge bunch of them from the display and to go sit in Iván and Eugenia's tiny shack in front of their TV and stuff myself with as much of that forbidden fruit as I could fit in my stomach. There were a lot of bananas, and this stunt landed me in bed for several days with a hepatitis scare. It marked the end of my visits to the produce market for quite some time, and when I finally returned it was for other reasons, and my old complicity with Iván and Eugenia was gone. But the memories remain forever, and Eugenia and Iván deserve their place in these pages, a place as solid as the one they hold in my heart.

First impressions to the contrary, or at least contrary to what I assume most people might think, there was no absence of political discussion in my house. Every Tuesday for as long as I can remember, we faithfully turned on the evening news with Bernardo Neustadt, a journalist with die-hard sympathies toward whatever government happened to be in power, especially if it was conservative or military. His program *Tiempo Nuevo* (New Times) is still so present in my mind that every time I hear the theme song, "Fuga y Misterio," I think more of Neustadt, who died in 2008, than of Astor Piazzolla, who composed it.

At the thought of sitting side by side with Raúl every Tuesday watching *Tiempo Nuevo*, I'm reminded of an episode that aired in 1994, during the presidency of Carlos Menem, who provoked a rapturous response from Neustadt. Back then, with pardons being issued for the military high brass and with the country submerged in a politics of "reconciliation with the past" imposed by the government, human rights associations were portrayed by programs such as Neustadt's as pariahs and destabilizing elements. Before us on the screen we saw the twins Matías and Gonzalo Reggiardo Tolosa in all their suffering.

Their story had begun in 1985, when, thanks to a tip from a North American journalist, the Grandmothers of the Plaza de Mayo finally located the probable children of Juan Reggiardo and María Tolosa, who were both *desaparecidos*. The children had been kidnapped during the dictatorship by Samuel Miara, a torturer and subcommissioner of the Federal Police. He moved with them to Paraguay, and after extradition orders and legal decisions, in 1993 the courts determined that the children should have their identity restored and be known by their original names. But too many years had elapsed since the beginning of the legal process, and by the time the order was handed down the boys were teenagers, which made their situation more traumatic. They were still very attached to their abductors, and their relationship with their blood family got off to a poor start.

When the judge heard their case, he decided that it would be best for Gonzalo and Matías to be returned to the family that had raised them. The worst tabloid papers, taking advantage of the fragility of two seventeen-year-olds, seized on the occasion to present the brothers as living proof of the cruelty of organizations such as the Grandmothers. The quest for justice and to restore the identity of two children who had been abducted at birth was instead portrayed as a thirst for revenge, and the abductors characterized as "loving parents" who had actually rescued the children from an even worse fate. Matías and Gonzalo petitioned the court to return to their former life so they could be with the couple they called "Papá" and "Mamá."

Remembering that case, I think of myself and my total lack of suspicion about my origin and identity, and wonder what would have happened if I had learned the truth while still an adolescent, when the person I am today was just beginning to take shape. If the word "abductor" still causes me pain at thirty-three, if my feelings toward my abductors are still ambiguous now, I don't know what would have happened then. I wish I could remember how I felt when I saw that program. I suppose more than anything I would have felt disgust at the spectacle of those two defenseless boys exposed to the cameras, and I would probably also have fallen into the trap of feeling sorry for them and hoping they'd be left in peace. Today I understand that the pain set in motion by the process of restitution is infinite and that it takes a different form in each case. Still, despite our differences, we all share this one point: our identity and roots are the first thing we receive in life, the first set of cards we're dealt. To deny someone those cards is to condemn him or her to a life without a stable foundation. The existence of people such as me or the twins or so many others is a direct consequence of state terrorism and its agenda of covering up the truth. For us to be able to exist, the truth has to be returned to us. To deny us our true identity can never be understood as a form of "protection." During Miara's trial, the prosecutor, Gustavo Bruzzone, said, "Not only did they illegally deprive the people they were fighting of their freedom and then destroy them, but they gave their children to families who would raise them with the values they claimed to be defending. They didn't just defeat them militarily; they also stole their children and robbed them of their history."

Argentina under President Menem (1989–1999) was in its heyday, yet the politics of human rights had simply vanished into the woodwork. We had been deemed part of the First

World, we were being offered imported goods on easy terms, and laws were passed that placed our peso and the dollar at parity. But at the same time, a huge segment of the population was being increasingly marginalized, jobs were growing scarcer, and Argentina's independence in political and economic terms had joined human rights at the bottom of the barrel.

I finished studying at Sacred Heart and we finally moved closer to the city and to Raúl's greengrocery, to Bernal, in the *partido* of Quilmes in Buenos Aires Province. We now lived in a house with an enormous courtyard filled with grass, where I spent many summers. A new chapter was beginning. I was starting middle school, still in a religious institution, but an all-girls one this time. Still unaware of the truth, I was embarking on a fairly traumatic adolescence in which I continued to exhibit a personality with certain "inexplicable" traits and to feel different from everybody else. Although I was still incapable of finding the reason why something always seemed either to be lacking in my daily life or to be present in excess, I increasingly felt that there was something inside me struggling to push its way out, and that my concerns could not be reduced to the typical conflicts of adolescence.

It was definitely during my transition from childhood to adolescence that I felt as never before that my life and my very being were out of sync, but I had no way to explain it until fifteen years later, when my true identity was revealed to me. Among all the traumatic facts that can emerge when someone like me learns the truth, one of the most painful and hardest to talk about has to do with my age. My mother was approximately five months pregnant when she was kidnapped at the Morón station in March 1977. Given the lack of exact information about what happened in the following months or even during the months leading up to her capture, the only evidence that enables me to reconstruct that part of my story are the accounts of survivors, a kind of jigsaw puzzle with many missing pieces. Trying to be as flexible as possible based on incomplete information, I can place my birth in the "maternity clinic" at the ESMA sometime between the months of July and September 1977. Yet when I was registered under the name Analía, all my documents gave my date of birth as September 17, 1979. Two years later.

The consequences were not simply that I spent my childhood believing that I was some kind of genius because I learned everything so fast, or that adolescence hit me much earlier than my friends and I felt my body leap ahead while my mind still wanted to keep playing like a child . . . No. The most violent effect, and the weight I still find most difficult to bear, is that even today I feel that the price I had to pay in order to have access to my real identity was to lose two years along the way, two years that no one, ever, can restore to me. For some reason, that loss is more painful for me to face than the lie of the people who called themselves my parents. As if I had awakened from a virtual coma, from one day to the next, two years of my life were simply erased.

In the midst of all my questions and my physical transformation, and just as we moved to a new house, I entered the

Institute of Young Ladies of the Sacred Family. It was then that I experienced my first real doubts about society and the world in which I was living, and about the lack of justice as history moved forward, trampling anyone in its path. Soon I would have to prepare for my confirmation, and I would discover that, beyond my life with its little circle of certainties, there was a vast universe of marginalized people, of social classes, and of structural differences that made it impossible for some people to even dream of changing the hand of cards they had been dealt.

Although I couldn't know it at the time, a new era had begun in which my mother was growing ever more present inside me, with her character, her explosiveness, and, little by little, her ideas and convictions.

My adolescence was beginning, and with it Victoria was rising to the surface in Analía. The moment of my inheritance had arrived.

# A New Beginning

With our move to the neighborhood of Bernal, in the municipality of Quilmes, we were that much closer to the city of Buenos Aires. Not only had we advanced within the concentric circles that surround the capital; we had also moved up a rung on the social ladder that separated us from the economic center of the country. We had left behind our apartment in a neighborhood of look-alike buildings, and could now lay claim to a whole house, whose grassy courtyard would gradually become an oasis in the desert of our Buenos Aires summers.

I entered the Institute of Young Ladies of the Sacred Family in 1991. The nuns continued to define the rhythm of my education, but from now on everything would unfold within an entirely female universe, with all the advantages and disadvantages such a realm implies. All around me, not just in Argentina but in the larger world, the values and ideas that had nourished us for decades were crashing to the ground with the same impact, and just as much noise, as the Berlin Wall had made when it fell two years earlier. Under President Carlos Menem, Argentina entered a new era in which the priorities were reform of the state apparatus, "national reconciliation," and improving the buying power of ordinary Argentines. To achieve this, the government

53

adopted neoliberal measures, dictated point by point by international financial organizations. A policy of privatization was introduced in which the operating principle was shame: corruption, the emptying of state-owned enterprises, massive layoffs, and, above all, frivolity. More or less echoing the pronouncements of the philosopher Francis Fukuyama, Menem declared to anyone who cared to listen that we had arrived at the end of ideology. The resulting death of values was the perfect excuse for runaway personal enrichment and lavish parties in which politicians, film stars, and opportunists of every stripe came together under one roof. Within a few short years, the national airlines, the state oil, gas, and water companies, and the Argentine telephone service along with the electrical companies were all put on the block, and countless other services previously backed by the government were allowed to fall into private hands. Such deals were consummated through the familiar pattern of insider tips and bribes, or simply via prior arrangement. The ranks of government now included such sinister characters as the Alsogaray family, Roberto Dromi, Carlos Corach, Domingo Cavallo, and, above all, President Menem himself, who grew more and more popular because of his participation in a range of sporting events, his obsession with cars, and his love for the shapeliest and most opportunistic women of Argentina and from around the world. The government was one endless party, and the president of Argentina was the most envied playboy in the country.

The rest of the world was hardly in better shape: the old Communist bloc was shattering, and the former Soviet republics were declaring independence until soon the Soviet Union itself had ceased to exist; then, using Saddam Hussein's invasion of Kuwait as an excuse, the United States declared war on Iraq, which lit the spark for the first Gulf War; the Italian Communist Party, the leading Communist party in the West, officially dissolved itself; and the Balkan wars got under way, with the resulting war crimes trials that are now before tribunals. The structures that had held for decades were crumbling, the old social, collective values were disappearing with giant steps, and a new era of individualism had been ushered in that gave no sign of yielding. That was the world of my early adolescence, a world adrift. And those were the events that began to sow the first seeds of doubt in my mind and make me wonder whether what was taking place around me was just or not.

In 1991, on orders from the secretary of the treasury, Domingo Cavallo, the Law of Convertibility established parity between the new Argentine peso and the dollar. Having finally brought the hyperinflation of the preceding years under control, the country entered a golden age in which the middle class was finally able to indulge its pent-up material desires, with trips abroad and the indiscriminate purchase of household appliances and imported goods, since tariffs had been eliminated. This period also saw the country's impoverished masses slowly march toward the abyss, a process that would hit the middle class ten years later and demolish the fragile, fictitious structure that, for one brief moment, seemed to signal that Argentina had irrevocably joined the First World.

In the meantime, while everything around me was shaking, my inner world was also in tumult, and with equally destructive force. As I've already mentioned, the problem of the two missing years between my real life and the one assigned to me by all my official papers is one I still have a hard time resolving. It was precisely during my early years as a teenager that this all came to the fore. At times the difference between what I was feeling and what was going on in my body, and what I was theoretically supposed to feel and what was supposed to happen to me physiologically, was simply unbearable, and my mood swings were as notorious as my precocious development. Throughout that whole time of heightened hormonal activity, I remember feeling unduly sensitive to things, like a sponge that soaks up every drop of water. Those were the years leading up to my confirmation in a little church a few blocks away from our new house.

The period of my preparation for my confirmation and the confirmation itself survive as fragments held together by external events that give them a larger meaning. I no longer remember, for example, the name of the priest who led our catechism classes, but I remember perfectly how much I hated him, and how afraid I was of him. He was the incarnation of what most teenagers would consider "old": thin, tall, stooped, and very bald, with little patches of wispy gray hair. To me he was a thousand years old, which meant he was easily sixty, although what bothered me most, even more than the wrinkles that furrowed his entire face except for the corners of his lips, was his extreme thinness. He was not just skinny, nor was this the sign of some asceticism on his part; his body was dried out and lifeless, like a thing overcome by bitterness. As can be imagined, we didn't have the best relationship. I did my part with my big mouth, which was increasingly hard to control. There again was Cori, although it was too early for me to recognize her in myself, arguing against every point that sounded too definitive to me, and offering my own absolutist declarations in response.

My relationship with that priest became so awful that one day, with the help of an accomplice, I decided to go on the attack. I would weaken my enemy by spreading false rumors about him, with the goal of undermining his position in the Church. I hadn't thought through the second half of the plan, but the first part was under way: we decided to spread a rumor that he was selling drugs to the neighborhood girls. This was another era—today, we would probably have accused him of running after boys. In any case, a rumor like that would suffice to spread a veil of doubt over this man of the cloth, forcing him into retirement. Then they would bring in someone younger, more handsome, and more entertaining. All we had to do was wait. And wait. Just a little longer.

Nothing came of it, of course. My plan to triumph in the art of war by employing a coldly calculated strategy against the enemy died with the first battle, and the worst of it was that no one knew but me. At least I learned that individuality was not for me, and that my increasingly combative tendencies would have to find another escape valve that made better use of them. My experience in church actually helped in that regard, particularly my participation in the youth group.

When the state is reduced to its most minimal expression, as happened with Argentina at the time, the Church ends up taking charge of social welfare and community work, especially in the poorest neighborhoods and slums. Small parishes function as de facto community centers, and many of the organizational aspects of neighborhood life revolve around them. My church youth group spent several hours a week, and especially our weekends, helping kids with homework, distributing food donations, and providing other social services in the poorest areas of the city. I was able to see with my own eyes the consequences of a globalized Argentina. We were talking no longer about structural problems, but about the collapse of the entire scaffolding of the state, from its basic humanitarian functions to its mechanisms of containment. It all happened so fast that the partisans of economic self-sufficiency didn't have time to analyze the situation of those who were left outside the narrow circle of profits. We taught senior citizens to read who had never had the chance to go to school and we tutored their grandchildren, who should have been in school but who, because they were either too poor to go, or too malnourished or even worse, still didn't know the alphabet.

Those solidarity projects with my church group were not my first contact with poverty and exclusion. I'd like to be able to say that I wasn't born with a silver spoon in my mouth, but given the circumstances, the phrase sounds odd at best. Still, the family that raised me wasn't rolling in money; and where we lived when I was little, the poverty all around us could hardly be ignored. What was new to me was finding a way to channel my indignation. Despite the fact that I still had no political awareness, I could actually do something, however small my contribution. And I felt useful.

It bears saying that what I discovered through this social and community involvement was that beyond its being the antithesis of my pathetic attempts to wage war against that horrible priest, I had a natural inclination toward this kind of work, however apolitical it was at first. This had nothing to do with the kind of satisfaction a rich person might feel by helping someone in need and thereby filing the rough edges of his bourgeois guilt. Nor was this a case of Christian charity. What I felt when doing this work was the sensation of doing something genuine, which showed me that there was a form of solidarity that could actually make a difference. On the days when I took part in these parish activities, during these moments of material and human exchange with people in need, I didn't feel good about myself or at peace with God—I simply felt useful. Of course I recognize that nothing is black or white, and that in the infinite universe of gray tones that constitute our existence, my motivation to continue my involvement went well beyond my relationship with God or with solidarity work. The smile that appeared on my face every time I walked from my house to the church had a name: it was Hernán.

Hernán was the coordinator of our youth group. He was twenty-three years old while I was only fifteen, and, best of all, he had a car. It's strange how such banalities could have been so important to me then, but the fact is that before his face, his voice, or his body, the first thing that comes back to me after all these years is the white Honda in which he drove me everywhere. I felt like a princess, or at least like a rich girl with a chauffeur. For a time, in the endless tug of war between my repulsion toward the priest and the satisfaction I derived from our solidarity work, Hernán tipped the balance that kept me going to church.

But just as a car can make all the difference to a teenager, the objects of her affection can be short-lived and changeable; it wasn't long before Hernán was no match for the Herculean task of shoring up my motivation when faced with catechism classes. Not to mention the fact that my relationship with the other girls in the group was so bad that it wasn't really a relationship, and that my accomplice in the attempt to bring down the priest had stopped going to church. All that was left for me to do was stop going too. Despite my explosive character, I'm not a woman who breaks ties easily. I need to take things step by step.

I began by signing up for theater courses at the local Italian cultural center, where I not only found an outlet for my dramatic tendencies but also fell madly in love with my teacher, although he never so much as looked my way. Still, along with my growing interest in the theater and my progressive alienation from the Church, this passion was sufficient to make Hernán absurdly jealous. By the time cars had lost their hold on my imagination and his jealousy had become acidic and possessive, it was time to end the whole adventure. When Hernán and his white Honda were no longer on the horizon, my battle with the horrible priest was over: soon afterward I left the youth group, and with that I left behind my first real experience of solidarity work.

It would be several more years before I decided to become politically involved, but the road ahead was clear. From that point on, Cori would never abandon me. She would remain an invisible guiding force within me and in my way of seeing things. Everything that happened next was part of the necessary process of finally opening my eyes and shaping what would evolve into my true vocation. The place where this slow transformation occurred was hardly a novelty: the Institute for Young Ladies of the Sacred Heart, where hundreds of girls between the ages of twelve and eighteen coexisted for the better part of the day with nuns, priests, and a handful of lay people in the sort of strict, repressive atmosphere only a religious school is able to create.

My initial impulse when I first arrived had been to seek out other girls like me, from middle-class families. I entered adolescence firmly in the grip of superficiality, obeying the rules of my little group without hesitation and without even thinking there might be another world not defined by mere appearances. The classroom where I spent my five years in the Institute was arranged in classic style: there were three double rows of desks in a square room with peeling yellow walls and large windows that faced the inner courtyard of the building. The geographic location of the desks determined which group one belonged to. Three rows, three groups. The first row, the one farthest from the doorway and facing the blackboard, was where I was placed in the beginning. We were the "popular" girls, the ones for whom all that mattered was fashion, boy talk (before we had actually met any boys), and vying to see who had the latest designer jeans or the shiniest kicks or the tightest tank tops—obviously our uniform outside of school, since by day we all had to wear the same black shoes, blue socks, blue dress, white blouse. With hair pulled back, of course. In my case, given my "problematic" and inexplicable early development, the tight-fitting camisoles only accentuated the difference in size that separated me from my classmates.

In the middle row were the girls who in every school in the world are classified as "nerds": those who study all the time, participate in class, and get the highest grades. Since these girls show a determined interest in their studies, they are automatically excluded from every possible social circle and are unable to shake off their pariah status until university, where everything begins anew. Meanwhile, for five long years, they form a solid, united block of girls who get together to study and have little contact with boys outside an academic context. For reasons unknown at least to me, they also tend to be unattractive, or at any rate so they are perceived, so much so that they generally see themselves that way too.

The third group, the one closest to the door, was defined more by its opposition to the other two than by any other common trait. The girls in this group were neither "popular" nor "nerds," but if we had to give them a name we would have called them "rebels" or "cool." They listened to local music, paid little attention to their clothes, and were neither sufficiently diligent in their studies nor sufficiently ugly to be put in the middle. The lives of these girls were defined completely outside school: by their friendships, their interests, and the places where they gathered socially. Theirs was the non-group group, the squaring of the circle that made it impossible to assign a strict caste system within the classroom. Later on, my true friends would emerge from that group—the girls with whom I shared my deepest feelings, my crushes and disappointments in love, along with the inevitable doubts and problems that arise in an environment in which our hormones and limited experience slowly mold the personalities that will be ours for the rest of our lives. But I'm getting ahead of myself. For the time being, my life revolved around my clothes, our heartless, cruel criticism of others, and the sick competitive spirit among us.

Our week consisted of waiting for Friday so we could finally get rid of our school uniforms and change into our other ones. Buenos Aires, the city that never sleeps, along with its outlying neighborhoods, has endless sources of entertainment for all ages, which meant that from early adolescence a girl so inclined could feel like an adult and go dancing at "matinées" that began at seven o'clock and ended at ten, the unofficial curfew for girls under eighteen. The nerve center of our group was a well-known discotheque in Quilmes, the Electric Circus. There, along with my "friends," I shook and swayed my then corpulent body standing on top of a huge speaker, showing off and watching everybody else show off just like me, all of us in a kind of trance induced more by our desire to seem older than by any real effect of the electronic music that was hammering in our ears. I wasn't the only daughter from a military family, nor the only girl whose ideas ran along similar lines to her origins. The boys we usually went out with and with whom we spent our weekends were mostly students at a technical trade school that prepared them for careers as airplane mechanics, which was under the direct control of the Argentine Air Force. The boys who went there were also from military families or at least had some connection to the Armed Forces. They were all middle class, and all of us were influenced by an ideology that viewed members of the military as heroes, as the guarantors and pillars of the values of God and Fatherland. It was a rancid world that either knew nothing of or was willing to distort Argentina's recent history, a history that had determined my existence in ways I still had no way of understanding.

By this point my rebellious, nonconformist spirit was pretty well defined, but I was still heavily influenced by what I heard at home, comments such as Raúl's contemptuous dismissal of the "atheist, unpatriotic Left." It wasn't until my second year of junior high that I had my first encounter with a reality different from the one I had always known. That year the first of what I call my external influences entered my life. Her name was Silvia, and she was my second-year teacher. She was short and pretty, with long blond hair. She was young, she was natural, and I hung on her every word. To my eyes she was beautiful. It was the first time I believed someone who presented me with a different idea of what had happened in Argentina, and of the role that people such as Raúl had played under the dictatorship.

It all came together during one of those countless patriotic school events we have in Argentina around the national holidays. Maybe July 9, for Independence Day, or May 25, for the commemoration of the first government assembly in 1810, or on some other special occasion when we all assembled in the central courtyard to sing the national anthem, the hymn to the flag, or any of the other hymns that are rolled out in Argentina to increase patriotic feelings within the student population. As always, my theatrical persona and ability to perform meant I had been asked to write a speech that I would read in front of everyone. I had grown to feel quite comfortable with my notoriety, and apparently all my teachers agreed this was the right role for me to play.

I no longer recall the subject, nor in fact do I remember much else of what took place that day, except the last line of my speech, no doubt heavily influenced by Raúl and his truths or half-truths, or what I would only later realize were out-and-out lies masquerading as the truth. Such as my date of birth. My name. My origin.

*And in the last war our glorious Argentine Army had to fight the godless enemy that knows no country, victorious and bathed in glory . . .*

Silvia, that marvelous creature whom I so revered, came up to me after my speech, and I immediately noticed her discomfort and her need to make me understand the exact meaning of those words. That day, for the first time, someone challenged the deeply rooted notion that what Argentina had fought was a "dirty war," in which two sides had clashed and from which one side had emerged victorious. Patiently, pedagogically, Silvia explained to me that wars are fought between states, between countries, or between factions, but that when one of the two sides is the state itself and the other is the people, then it's not a war but state terrorism. She also explained to me that the "godless" enemy I had invoked had come from within the Church, and that their leader was a priest who had inspired an entire generation in the struggle against oppression and injustice. This was Father Carlos Mugica, murdered by the Triple A for thinking differently. She told me how those I had called "unpatriotic" had their roots in Catholic nationalism, and that the difference between them and their murderers was their *patria*, the country for which they had fought the most entrenched structures of the state, which was simply a different idea of *patria*, a more just and sovereign one. And that our "glorious Argentine Army" had cemented its victory not through a battle between equals but through the disappearance, torture, and extermination of those it had deemed enemies.

I was very young for my teacher Silvia's words to be able to topple the house of lies in which "my" ideas had taken root, or to make me completely question the ideology of Raúl, who was still the most important man in my life. But this was the first thrust, the first hint that something more lay beyond the affirmations of my "father." How could someone be glorious if the glory of his victory was built on hate, intolerance, and unbridled violence? I still wasn't ready to oppose the version of history on which I had been raised, but I could no longer reconcile the word "justice" with what Silvia had told me.

By this point it was impossible to deny that something new had begun to move inside me. I could no longer hold it back. Of course the daily contradictions in my life persisted, and for a while longer I managed to combine my growing rebellion and my superficial relationships with the other girls in the "popular" group. But the seed that had been planted continued to grow after Silvia's respectful, convincing conversation, and began to take hold in everything I did.

Through a combination of internal and external influences, I was beginning to constitute myself as an individual with her own ideas. But even if for the moment I could not have put a name to the force that was struggling to emerge in my blood and in my true history, the outside influences on me were and remain easy to identify. The first was my experience helping those most marginalized by the economic system that ruled Argentina in the 1990s, whether as the kind of Christian charity that Church doctrine required or as an act of social construction based on the simple concept of denying that poverty and inequality were unavoidable. The second influence was Silvia, the beautiful young teacher who was closer in age to me than she was to the priests and nuns and who managed to guide me into a process of reflection strong enough to erase the word "undeniable" from the political discourse I drank in every day at home. The third was someone who helped me fill in the cracks and holes that had opened up once I no longer accepted the "givens" on which I had been raised. That someone was Luis, the priest who administered confession to all the girls at Sacred Heart.

Among the numerous rules of conduct and appearance the nuns laid down was the requirement to wear our hair pulled back. I usually tied mine badly, so the knot would slowly loosen over the course of the day and a few strands of my long, wavy hair would escape, if only briefly. The nuns' constant comments about this, and my increasingly overwhelming need to question every aspect of their control, led to my being "punished" with alarming frequency. The punishment was invariably to reflect and repent, which meant being sent to Father Luis. He was about thirty years old, tall, and rather overweight, and I never saw him without the white clerical collar that defined his role in the Institute. I imagine he would have preferred not to wear such a uniform, which positioned him a rung above the girls who came to see him, but he too was subject to the school's iron-clad rules. When Father Luis was speaking to someone, he rarely looked at them; instead, his green eyes were lost in some distant corner of the horizon, which gave him the calm to express himself clearly and without a trace of arrogance. Despite the rules and traditions that were so important to the nuns, Father Luis had managed to break down certain structures, so that confession with him did not take place in a little box with a perforated screen between us, nor shut within the four walls of his office or the chapel, but by going out for a walk. If you went to confess with Father

Luis you would stroll together through the garden, talking about whatever had led to your visit or simply about history, life, or anything else you wanted to bring up. He understood better than anyone the role of a confessor: someone in whom you could confide with the knowledge that nothing you told him would ever escape and who, instead of imposing his opinions, freely offered them in order to encourage you to expose your own.

I had a history teacher who taught us the history of Argentina in the purest style of heroes and villains, a history that could be discussed only from an "official" point of view that allowed no room for questions. Still, he sometimes slipped from his role as the all-knowing one and encouraged us to investigate things for ourselves and develop our own thoughts, even if in the end it was only to debunk any differences of opinion as false. One day, in the middle of a lecture, he proposed that we stage a mock trial of one of the most controversial figures of the nineteenth century, Juan Manuel de Rosas. Rosas is widely seen as a classic *caudillo*, a violent dictator who was heroically toppled by his archenemy, Justo José de Urquiza, who represented European liberalism at its most illustrious. But in a vision born of the popular classes of Argentina, Rosas can also be seen as one of the first politicians to approach the people who were pushed aside as the country was being built, which is to say the "gauchos," who symbolized barbarism to the thinkers of the period. For many, including Father Luis, Rosas belonged to a kind of Holy Trinity of Argentine history alongside General San Martín, the founding father of the country, and Juan

Domingo Perón. I no longer remember whether my role in that fictitious trial of Rosas was that of defense lawyer or prosecutor, but I do remember my surprise and frustration when I realized that in the different books I consulted as I prepared my argument, the same acts were presented by some as unforgivable crimes and by others as heroic deeds. On my walks through the school gardens with Father Luis, I came to understand that history is not an unquestionable truth but an analysis of events that took place in the past, which can be read only through the eyes of the present. He never tried to indoctrinate me with his personal vision; he simply presented it to me as yet another option, and as proof that the only person with the right to shape my opinion was myself.

Father Luis also taught me that it is precisely because we are able to construct our own opinions that we should fight to defend them, without imposing them on others, but also without allowing anyone to impose on us what we should feel or think. It was he who gave me my first lesson in politics, and the book that allowed me to mold my influences to my actions: the *Complete Works of Ernesto "Che" Guevara*, which continues to be the primary source of inspiration for my political activity. Che lived and thought in the same manner, without contradictions, taking his beliefs to the extreme of giving his life for them. If I ever create a Holy Trinity of my own, I know that Che Guevara will be part of it.

There is no such thing as a straight line in a person's existence. Events don't lead one to the next in perfect harmony, but rather collide and overlap in a chaos of opposing forces that shape our personal story and don't acquire significance until they can be read as part of our past. And just as I can affirm while I write this that Cori, my mother, was already alive within me, and that her genes and blood were molding my character with a force equal to that of the external elements that were marking my life, these external elements can be separated and identified only from the prism of the present. The reality back then was that Silvia, my social involvement through the Church, Father Luis, Che Guevara and his *Complete Works*, even Hernán and his imported white car and my drama workshops were all happening at the same time as my puberty, as my involvement with various groups, as my dancing on top of the speakers at the Electric Circus on Saturday nights, as my flirtations with future military mechanics. The person who put on her makeup and excitedly untied her hair the second she got out of school each afternoon was the same one who would have it out with Raúl because she wanted to hang a poster of Che on the door of her room. We are all several things at once. We are all inhabited by contradictions and opposing forces that win and lose the game by turns. What is it, then, that gives a different color to my story, and that makes those moments of my life worth retelling? I was still called Analía, my father was a retired member of the Argentine police, I was born in 1979. But I was also always Victoria, the daughter of Cori and El Cabo, born in 1977 in a concentration camp in the middle of Buenos Aires. My true life did not begin at twenty-seven, just as everything that happened to me before that time cannot be defined as a mere lie. In this sense my story does not belong only to me, to Victoria or Analía, but is the story of Argentina, a story of intolerance, violence, and lies the consequences of which we're still living with today. It's a story that won't be complete until the last of the babies abducted during the dictatorship has recovered its identity, until the last of those responsible for that act of barbarism is tried for his crimes, until all the thirty thousand disappeared have names, until their history and the full circumstances of their deaths are known, until the last of their relatives can finally mourn. As was the case with me and with those who preceded me, and as will be the case with those who come after, the truth always rises, forcing its way up through the edifice of lies and subterfuges constructed over so many years. My story, then, is not mine alone but belongs to everyone. It is the modest contribution I allow myself to make in order to shed even a little bit of light on the truth.

And so, with that whole pile of contradictions and events that were slowly influencing and determining my behavior, and thanks to the possibility of relativizing things that I learned from my conversations with Father Luis, I began to distance myself from everything I had considered fundamental in determining how I defined myself: slowly, designer jeans, going dancing, and the competitions among my friends to see who could eat less began to lose their importance until I finally came to see them as superficial attitudes devoid of meaning. Whether because of the typical rifts that occur in a group of teenagers in the middle of high school, lack of interest, or both, I slowly moved away from the tightly knit group that sat on the left side of the classroom and began to acquire new interests and new friends. For the very reasons that defined it, the third, more amorphous group composed of those who didn't fit in either of the others now became mine: we didn't all have to be exactly the same; we could identify ourselves based on our differences. From then on I would never belong to a whole group but to people in general, and above all to individuals whose dissimilarities created the possibility of true friendship.

My real name, the one my mother had given me and that defined me for the short two weeks I spent at her side before they murdered her, took on its full significance at that point in my life. Not by imposing itself on top of Analía, nor by replacing her, but by forging her character, and thus preparing the terrain in which the two of us could coexist. This is why when my true origin was revealed to me years later, I was able to accept it with the certainty of a person who knows that the point was not to be two people at once, Analía and Victoria, but that those two people, those two names, and those two histories were already merged into one: myself.

# Definitions

The 1990s will forever be etched in the memory of Argentines as "Menem's decade." Those were the years of my entire secondary education and my first two years of university. As soon as he was elected president in 1989, Carlos Menem implemented a multifaceted assault on hyperinflation that included privatizing state enterprises, establishing currency controls under the Law of Convertibility, eliminating price controls, and deregulating imports. Two years into his term, with the ascent of Domingo Cavallo, who would be his star treasury secretary, the application of these policies began to create a false sense of prosperity. This was supported by easy access to credit for the middle classes and by improving certain formerly public services that were now privately run (primarily telephone, television, and electricity). The country's economic progress was marked by the growing gap between rich and poor, and the nation's indices of unemployment and debt continued to rise year after year. The critical moment of Menem's honeymoon can probably be placed at the end of 1994, the year of his constitutional reform.

Aside from a few minor changes, the Argentine Constitution dates from 1853, when presidential terms were set at six years and were made unrenewable. Determined to remain in power, and buoyed by highly favorable public opinion,

Menem and the main opposition party jointly launched a process known as the "Olive Pact," a national plebiscite that led to the reform of the constitution and allowed him to run for a second term.

The year 1995 found the country with a new constitution and a flamboyant president who had just been reelected to a new four-year term. Everything was in place for a huge celebration, but the government, blinded by its zeal to remain in power and victim of the unprecedented frivolity that had played a direct role in Menem's reelection (as the best-dressed politican in the world), did not anticipate the consequences of what would later become known as the "Tequila Crisis." When the Mexican government devalued their peso at the end of 1994, restructuring their financial system, they triggered a regional economic crisis that quickly engulfed Argentina. Despite maintaining parity between the Argentine peso and the dollar and keeping a lid on inflation, the country's banking system collapsed, provoking a recession that would last for several years and that would disproportionately affect the usual suspects: those already struggling to survive. Unemployment reached 20 percent among the working-age population. Argentina was forced to continue accruing debt in order to meet the payment deadlines of its prior obligations, applying ever more draconian measures and pushing vast sectors of the population deeper into a poverty from which they have yet to emerge.

This was the context in which I spent my middle school and high school years: in a country that had cozied up to the tenets of neoliberalism, which held that ideology of any stripe was dead and that individualism trumped any form of solidarity across class lines. Within that framework of "each man for himself," after spending my middle school years doing community service in old people's homes and orphanages that were a textbook illustration of the country's situation, I couldn't help but begin to question the kind of life I had carved out for myself.

But it's also true that I was only fifteen, and it would be unfair to cloak the complex process of adolescence as purely a political coming-of-age. Even though I had grave doubts about my circle of friends and was growing more cynical by the day about their prevailing superficial ideals, once again the determining factor in my break with the popular girls was probably, as was by now my custom, a man. I no longer recall the exact facts, but it all came to a head when a boyfriend of one of the girls decided to fall in love with me, a situation, I should say, I did little to discourage. The fight with the other girls was visceral, like everything else at the time, and the end result was that without really seeking it, I found myself suddenly free of their clutches. By that point I had managed to cultivate a few other friendships, most of all with the girl who would be my best friend up until we both entered university: Fernanda.

Fernanda was not just my physical but also my aesthetic opposite: she was blond, with green eyes and dark skin, but lighter than mine, and she was thinner. She was the incarnation of "cool" Argentine youth, which we called "stone," after the Rolling Stones. In my mind's eye she's dressed entirely in black, from her Topper sneakers, the mythic Argentine brand of sportswear, to her torn jeans and the eternal T-shirts that bore the names of her favorite bands: Guns N' Roses, Patricio Rey and his Redonditos de Ricota, Sumo, the indispensable Rolling Stones, and, of course, Los Caballeros de la Quema, which became our favorite group. No matter where they played, we followed them from concert to concert.

Once, in the middle of the summer, Fernanda appeared in my front yard to convince me to go with her to hear Los Caballeros de la Quema in Hurlingham, which was at the extreme opposite end of Buenos Aires. To get there, we had to take a train all the way to Constitución and then catch a bus that would get us closer to the concert. It was so hot out that the light was almost white and burned your skin as if the fire of the sun were just a few yards away. With the temperature hovering near ninety degrees in the shade, the never-ending humidity of summer made it feel more like a hundred.

I was cutting the grass and tanning myself in preparation for our annual vacation at the beach. When you're going to the beach you have to arrive already tanned in order to roast in the sun like a lizard and get darker by the end of the holiday; turning red as a shrimp is the best recipe for being ostracized.

"The Caballeros are playing in two hours in Hurlingham," she said by way of greeting, without even looking at me.

"Where's Hurlingham?"

"I have no idea. Near Luján, I think."

That was good enough for me. I knew in a flash that I didn't have enough information to convince Raúl to give me permission, so I just pulled a shirt and a pair of shorts over my bikini, threw my keys, money, and ID into a fanny pack, and followed Fernanda off on our adventure. Two hours later we were standing in front of the stage, a few feet away from Iván Noble, the lead singer of the band, and jumping and screaming like two souls possessed and singing along:

| | |
|---|---|
| *Apuesto al Quijote aunque ande rengo.* | I swear by Don Quixote even if he's lame, |
| *Brindo por tipos sin antifaz.* | I drink to the men without masks, |
| *Me abrazo a la rabia de los vencidos* | I embrace the rage of the vanquished |
| *Que Cruzan sin mapas la oscuridad.* | Who traverse the dark without maps. |
| *Hasta estallar.* | Till they explode. |
| *Hasta estallar.* | Till they explode. |

Everything would have been perfect if not for the fact that the concert was as long as it was amazing and that we had to go home the way we had come. It was three o'clock in the morning and we were two fifteen-year-old girls, both scantily clad, waiting for a train at Constitución, one of the most dangerous stations in the city. We were both scared out of our minds, but we tried our hardest to look as brave as possible to reduce our panic. But what terrified me most was the vision of what would happen when I got home, since I had left without telling anyone.

We got home—very late, and with our tails between our legs. The rage I had imagined from Raúl was in fact relief at seeing me alive, as would be the case so many other times in my life. To write about Raúl, to recall him at those times when he was my father and I felt as if I were (and knew myself to be) the light of his eyes, his princess, brings back a painful wound that will never heal. For a daughter, or for a son, parents aren't people; they have no other life beyond their role as parents. For me, Raúl was my father, a businessman who had once been part of the police but whose opinions, which more and more opposed my own, were simply the result of the fact that he was old and I was young. Each of us thought the way we were supposed to. As a father, Raúl was devoted if distant, strict but just. And I, as his older daughter, knew exactly how to reach his weak spots, and how to get him to forgive the unforgivable, since I felt immensely loved and respected. Like the time he saw the poster of Che Guevara I had put up in the hallway, on my bedroom door, and instead of throwing a fit like a monster who couldn't abide "lefties," ripping it down, and refusing to give me food for days, he simply told me to put it on the inside of my door. Or when I shredded my designer jeans into rags by slicing them with a razor and he quietly said he wouldn't give me another cent to spend on clothes, a threat he forgot as soon as I next asked him. Or when he incredulously but silently watched me dress from head to toe in skulls, which I wore in rings, on necklaces, and printed on camisoles and scarves that I tied around my wrists and head.

If the ambiguity I feel today about my relationship with Raúl is bearable, if I'm able to have contact with him and Graciela without denying my true identity or the role they played in having me find out so late, it's above all because I was already an adult when I learned the truth. This meant that I could separate the Raúl of my memories from the Raúl who had been a torturer at the ESMA, a member of Operations Group 3.3.2, my abductor.

That same summer, Fernanda came with us to the beach at San Bernardo. By that point she was my absolute idol. Vacations were a time of greater freedom and a taste of real independence, since we were allowed to go dancing during regular night hours, instead of having to attend the infuriating "matinées" we were restricted to during the school year. One night, after buying platform shoes that added about eight inches to our height and had us hobbling around as if we were on stilts, we convinced Raúl to let us go out dancing with a curfew of 6:30 in the morning.

We weren't sure where to go, so we just followed the crowds of young people on the main drag, stumbling forward on our platforms until we found a suitable place to unload our pent-up urge for movement. We danced without a break until six o'clock in the morning, to an eclectic mix of summer disco music that combined national rock favorites, imitations of the latest trends in electronic music, and dubious entries from the summer hit parade. By the time we left the club the sun was coming up. As soon as we got outside we realized that we had taken a different door from the one we had gone in through, which dealt a serious blow to our shaky sense of direction. The only point of reference I could recall was a huge stationary blimp with the 7UP logo on the beach, where we needed to turn and walk another hundred yards to reach our house. But first we had to find the beach. In part because it was so late and in part because of how we were dressed, but above all because of my insistence on doing everything without help, neither Fernanda nor I had the slightest intention of making fools of ourselves by asking where the beach was. When we stumbled toward the edge of the water sometime later and could finally pull off our heavy astronaut's boots, the sun was high on the horizon and we began to look for the famous 7UP balloon. We walked and walked and eventually ran into two older boys who were playing beach ball.

Without paying any special attention to us, they began throwing the ball in the direction we were walking, appearing to follow us by chance and periodically talking to each other. It wasn't long before the four of us were walking side by side, without anybody asking where we were going or when we would arrive. Finally, after a long stretch during which we cracked jokes and talked, one of them asked if we were staying in San Bernardo or in Mar del Tuyú, which were several miles apart.

"San Bernardo—why?" I replied.

"Because we've just arrived in Mar del Tuyú. San Bernardo is that way."

Without realizing, we had walked in the exact opposite direction from the 7UP balloon, and to make matters worse, it was 8:30 in the morning, two hours later than the curfew Raúl had imposed as a condition of letting us go dancing.

We had to retrace our steps the whole way back, still accompanied by our two knights, who by this point had names: Jorge and Mariano. When we finally got home it was ten o'clock, and Raúl was waiting in front of the door with a policeman who had been summoned because of us.

We were grounded for the whole next day and several days and nights after. But Mariano and Jorge came to see us, and stood chatting with us outside the front door. At that moment a friendship was sealed with both boys, especially with Mariano, that would make this a turning point in my political development and pave the way for me to become a true activist.

I soon became close friends with Mariano and broke up with the boy who had cost me my niche in the clique of "popular" girls. My relationships with both Mariano and Jorge were among the most important of my teen years, in terms of friendship and romance. Mariano, Jorge, and their friends were from Solano, a working-class neighborhood in the district of Quilmes. They were three years older than Fernanda and me, and most of them had dropped out of high school to take jobs and devote themselves to music. Mariano was tall and thin, with long, straight black hair that was almost always wet, as if he had just stepped out of the shower. He was the singer of their band, and Fernanda, Nancy (my other new girlfriend), and I went to all his concerts and sang his songs just as we had sung and danced to Los Caballeros de la Quema.

Despite our supposed rebelliousness, through our musical taste and our way of dressing, the reality was that we were still teenage girls from a convent school, and our only contacts with men took place outside of school, which gave added luster to our new circle of friends. The three of us barely sipped a beer between us, while many of the boys drank and even used cocaine before their concerts, right in front of us, as if there was no reason to hide it. This sort of cultural difference led to a few clashes, and a couple of times they had to call a taxi to take me home when I couldn't put up with watching them heat a plate and snort that unfamiliar white powder.

But the differences among us were continually erased by our complicity and by the friendship I felt for Mariano and Jorge. In their company, this or that comment by my teacher Silvia or Father Luis's historical relativism went from being interesting perspectives to demands that I redefine myself. Mariano was young, passably poor, and a musician, and considered himself part of an apolitical yet somehow active left that was typical of the neoliberal years in Argentina, when the much vaunted "death of ideology" seemed to authorize those in power to engage in every manner of democratic abuse. My own ambiguous political line, in which a degree of social consciousness coexisted with a fierce defense of the police and Armed Forces, was barely tenable when I was forced to confront its flagrant contradictions.

My new awareness distanced me from the political climate that prevailed at home, and while Raúl and I continued to share an interest in politics and in the shifts of

Argentine political life, a kind of no-man's-land opened up between us, in which an increasing number of subjects became taboo. That was when I began to pay real attention to stories of the country's recent past, even though I was still incapable of imagining how much they had to do with me. Raúl continued to support the idea of a "dirty war," in which two opposing sides had clashed: on the one hand, the army, the last bastion and guarantor of Christian, national values, and on the other, an army of revolutionaries who believed in neither God nor Fatherland. In that war, torture, disappearance, and the bodies tossed into the sea from army planes were all minimized to the point of being viewed simply as "excesses," which of course had been committed by both sides. His thinking didn't go much beyond that. In fact, because he was so vague and never spoke with any detailed information, I always assumed that his participation in that "dirty war" was anecdotal. Years later, when Raúl, whom I still thought of as my father, the father of Analía, appeared on the list of men whose extradition for alleged crimes of torture and murder had been requested by the Spanish judge Baltasar Garzón, it was like a bucket of cold water thrown in my face and as much of a fathomless shock as it was when, three months later, I learned my true identity.

But that sinister and at the same time liberating future was still a way off, and for now my friendship with Mariano and Jorge continued to flourish. Thanks to them I was able to further the social awareness I had developed during my school years and to understand that helping people doesn't go far enough to bring about real change. I realized that actions have to go hand in hand with speaking out, with a strong, clear protest that gives voice to our discontent.

In a sense, it's as if Mariano and Jorge showed me a way to channel the inner strength of Cori, my mother, who was struggling to find her way to the surface. In my conversations with Mariano, in his way of never letting me get away without justifying every assertion, Cori was leading me along a path of growth, and guiding my rebellious character and my need to question everything toward a place in which it would acquire a meaning, a mission, and an idea of justice. While it would be much later before I would discover aspects of my father in my need to take on political responsibilities and my seriousness in going about them, my mother had been boiling inside me always, and in the only way she knew how: in the midst of chaos. Just up ahead of me, although I couldn't see her, Cori was no longer dragging along her heavy duffel bag filled with weapons and shouting "Bastards!" She was turning around and smiling at me, waiting for me to follow her.

So, in the midst of my endless conversations and exchanges with Mariano and Jorge, my bulletproof friendship with Fernanda, and my need to begin to do something concrete with my political leanings and my desire to make a difference, I was coming to the end of high school. During my last and senior year in the Institute of the Sacred Family, I began to look at my options for university with an eye to embarking on the Ciclo Básico, the first year of study that provides the foundation for all subsequent careers at the University of Buenos Aires. I was torn between sociology, which seemed a better fit with my dawning social awareness, and the law, a kind of flexible career that would let me be a lawyer to make good money or to use it as a solid general foundation on which to build something else. Once again, taking the present as a way of reading into the past, there was another coincidence that makes me think that so much is determined by our genes: my mother had begun with sociology when she entered university, and my father had studied law. Both departments were housed at the time in the same building, the law school on Avenida Figueroa Alcorta, the same avenue that continues north to the door of the ESMA. As I faced these doubts about my choice of career, it was Raúl who once again played a decisive role. I think he was probably disgusted by the idea of having me study sociology in that "nest of leftists," so he offered me two nonnegotiable choices. If I wanted law, it would be at the University of Buenos Aires. If I wanted sociology, then he would enroll me in a private school that would guarantee there would be no brainwashing: the Catholic University of Argentina, which by the end of the 1990s had become one of the intellectual centers of the so-called Menemist intelligentsia.

Needless to say, I opted for law. I imagine that from wherever they were, Cori and El Cabo would have smiled not only to see their daughter hesitate between the two careers that they had chosen, but also because she would soon be going up and down the same corridors as they had, studying in the same classrooms, and becoming politically involved with a group that was fighting for the same ideals for which, in their time, they had given their lives.

Fernanda, meanwhile, had decided to study psychology. Thanks to her gravitations and her ability to convince me to follow her down every wild path she took, I found myself again doing community service. The need to make an active commitment to my political ideals grew stronger. It all began when I went with Fernanda to the psychology department to get orientation information on their programs, activities, and aspects of her chosen career. She happened to pick up a leaflet from the organization ABC Lo Cura, which was asking for volunteers to help reintegrate patients from the Borda, the largest psychiatric hospital for men in Buenos Aires, and probably in Argentina. I don't know how it happened, or the exact order of events, but when we left the building on Avenida Independencia, we both had a date for the following Monday in front of the main entrance to the Borda, where we would begin as volunteers.

The José Tiburcio Borda Neuropsychiatric Hospital is a gigantic fifteen-block complex located near the Constitución train station and filled with gardens and buildings that house various parapsychiatric institutes and research labs. More than one thousand men live inpatient at any time, and the facilities also treat roughly the same number on an outpatient basis. Founded during the second half of the nineteenth century, what was once one of the largest and most ambitious neuropsychiatric projects in Latin America is today a ruin whose buildings are barely standing, whose patients spend most of their time at the mercy of God for lack of staff, and where petty theft and aggression are the order of the day due to a complete lack of security.

As always when Fernanda was in the picture, we arrived late for our first volunteer session at the Borda. I don't know how she managed to do it, but even if she left hours ahead of time she was always late to her appointments. It was the middle of the winter in Buenos Aires, which meant that at eight o'clock, the time of our meeting, it was already pitch-black, without a star in the sky. We arrived chilled to the bone in our school uniforms, two noisy and terrified young girls trying to find the workshop we were supposed to take part in. When we finally found someone who could point us in the right direction, the security guard sent us to a far-off building where we had to walk down a long hallway. This corridor was poorly lit with dim fluorescent bulbs, but it was enough for us to see the dampness on the narrow, peeling walls and the seemingly endless series of doors that led to unknown rooms. At the end of the hallway there was a man leaning on the wall who stared at us while slowly moving his right index finger back and forth across his throat in an unmistakable slitting gesture. That first image turned out to be all too representative of the threatening atmosphere of the hospital once the sun went down and night fell.

I should state here that, despite Fernanda's indefatigable will, which allowed her to continue to take part in the rehabilitation workshops for several years to come, I lasted only a couple of months. I realized early on that the Borda was not the place for me to make a difference or to establish a link between my beliefs and actions. I never felt comfortable working there, and it made me profoundly sad to witness the constant impotence that set the rhythm of the hospital.

The truth is that I was afraid, and the best way for bad things to happen to a person is to be on guard against them. But the straw that broke the camel's back wasn't sadness; it was fear. One day while I played checkers with an outpatient in one of the immense hospital gardens, the patient took the opportunity to "crown" me by emptying a bowlful of popcorn on my head. Struggling to hold back tears, I left early that day, and that was the end of my job as a volunteer at the Borda. Fernanda reported the incident, but I said nothing. I preferred to fight on behalf of others, rather than for myself.

While I continued to look for a space in which to channel my interests and energy, I felt more and more identified with the character whom Father Luis had introduced me to by offering me his collected works: Che Guevara. While it's true that I first became acquainted with him through his writing, I also followed so many other young people in Argentina and around the world in connecting to him through his image. Besides the poster I put up inside my bedroom, I had added to my wardrobe a beret like the one he wore—I could barely be separated from it except to bathe and sleep. Naturally, that generated new tension with Raúl, who was by no means resigned to this latest twist on his daughter's ideological path.

But the worst was yet to come. When I finally began my classes at the University of Buenos Aires, many of them held in the same law school where I would later study, I found myself facing an interminable array of tables at the entrance, all manned by representatives of the various political parties and organizations that participated in the student center. The law school was a right-wing bastion at the time, and even the Franja Morada, the student branch of the center-left Unión Cívica Radical (UCR), had to adjust its positions to those of the silent majority that voted in the school. Among all the tables, with their flags, posters, flyers, and announcements from the leaders of political groups of every stripe, I managed to pick out the poster of Venceremos. Perhaps I was simply carried away by the huge Argentine flag with the figure of my beloved Che, or else it was the way their representative came over to me and offered me their publication, or the fact that he didn't try to explain their views to me but to discuss the reality of Argentina. I stopped at that table and listened to what they were saying, and I ended up spellbound by the work they were doing in the neediest areas of La Boca, a barrio on the southern edge of Buenos Aires. Venceremos, a student organization affiliated with the Patria Libre movement, considered itself a revolutionary, nationalist group and was opposed to the neoliberal policies of the government of Carlos Menem, which was in its death throes; to the international pressures that were suffocating the country in the form of an unpayable foreign debt; and to economic programs dictated by the same international organizations that held title to the debt.

It's not unusual for me to make the most transcendent decisions, the ones with the deepest implications, the ones whose consequences will resonate through the rest of my existence, without thinking very much or even thinking at all. If I had stopped at the time to think about what Raúl would have to say about my decision, if I had understood all that I would have to give of myself from that moment on, perhaps I would have continued on my way. But I had just made another frustrating attempt to get involved in community service by volunteering with patients at the Borda, and Che was gazing out at me from his flag as if he expected something more of me, so I immediately signed up as a volunteer in the community-based workshops the Venceremos group was holding.

My beginnings as an activist were anything but easy. It was one thing to be a rebel at home, to confront Raúl with my still-embryonic political ideas and to channel my energies through the good works of the church group or other NGOs. It was quite another to belong to a political movement with a clearly revolutionary left-wing line, and one that expected hours and hours of dedication as a sign of one's commitment. The first solution I came up with for avoiding a direct clash at home was simply to lie: in order to attend the Venceremos meetings and take part in the workshops in La Boca, I made up a church community-service program that worked in different neighborhoods around the city. For the first several months, this strategy worked, in part because my family seemed pleased that I was involved with a church again and was thus avoiding the evil influences of the University of Buenos Aires.

In the barrio of La Boca we organized homework clinics for kids, and as law students we also offered legal advice to those who could not afford to hire a lawyer. The organization under whose aegis all these activities were held was Students in Solidarity (Grupo de Estudiantes Solidarios), which was part of Venceremos. People in the neighborhood also chipped in with donations of bread, cookies, powdered milk, and other things that enabled us to offer the kids a snack when they arrived from school. At first we held our workshops in a neighborhood credit union, but they soon threw us out and we used the basement of a large local building. It was very demanding work, not only because of the number of hours it required but also because of the constant difficulty of having to face the extreme situations brought on by poverty. Day after day, everything was like having to begin from scratch, and every problem seemed insoluble at first. In such conditions, you needed to be highly motivated and sure of your convictions in order not to give up at the first obstacles. But that's where I was able to confirm what I had always suspected: if there was one thing I could count on, it was my motivation, which along with my stubbornness and the ties I gradually forged with my *compañeros* in the struggle, caused me to feel, for the first time, that I had finally found the path for my political activism.

From that moment on, activism became the center of my life: my studies, my extracurricular activities, my friendships, and even my enmities revolved around my political world. I count myself among those who believe that as we go through life we seek something that will give it meaning, something that will elevate our existence above the trinity of being born, reproducing, and dying. For me, that has been all the more true since I became involved with Venceremos. From the very first day, my political engagement became the defining axis of my life. When I learned the truth about my origins, when I found out who my parents were and that they had fought for the same goals I was fighting for myself, my activism became the raft that kept me from sinking, from falling apart like a marionette suddenly dropped by the puppeteer who had invisibly been moving it all along. Unlike so many other recovered grandchildren, when I learned the truth about my parents, their ideas and the reasons for their death, I didn't have to question an ideology I had been nursed on since the cradle that preached the wisdom of ideas such as the "dirty war." I had developed my own, choosing my influences and facing what had to be confronted. When I found out who my parents were I couldn't help but be proud of them, and I was sure that, somewhere, they were proud of me too.

But although it was drawing ever closer, the moment of the revelations hadn't yet arrived, and I had to resort to ever more complicated excuses to hide my activism from Raúl. When I think back to those years, when I remember the arguments we had about my Che beret or my attempts to convince him of the impossible, I remember someone else who played an important role in my growth, although I didn't see him often. This is the man I called "uncle," who I was told had been my godfather when I was baptized, a great friend of Raúl's from their days in the police. The man who religiously sent me birthday presents every year and who called me his "little brunette" the three or four times I saw him as a child and then later, when I was less docile and more combative, began to call me "lefty." My supposed godfather, the police officer Héctor Febrés. The man in charge of Section 4 at the ESMA, the improvised maternity wing where pregnant detainees gave birth before being murdered (or "transferred," as the army, with their cynical humor, preferred to call it). The man who tore me from my mother's arms.

My first abductor.

José María Donda—
my father—in suit and tie at
a school performance.

María Hilda Pérez, known as Cori, my mother. Shown here during her student years (third from left in the front row).

Cori at her *fiesta de quince años* (fifteenth birthday party).

Cori at sixteen, at the *quince años* of her sister Mary.

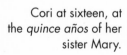

The Pérez family:
Mary, my grandfather
Armando, Tito,
my grandmother
Leontina, Inés, and
Cori, age 13.

My maternal
grandparents,
Armando and
Leontina, in a
family toast.

My paternal grandparents,
Cuqui and Telmo (on the right).

José María (center) with fellow students at the Naval Academy, 1972.

Cori Pérez and José María Donda, my parents.

Cori and José María on their wedding day, 1973.

The Sardá, or maternity clinic, of the ESMA, where female detainees gave birth. I was born in this tiny room.

Me, age 2.

In my high school days, at the Holy Family
Institute, 1994.

At my graduation ceremony, 1997.

The final national meeting of Patria Libre, in the Western Railway stadium of Buenos Aires.

With Humberto Tumini, general secretary of Libres del Sur, at the same event.

© Damián Neustadt

October 8, 2004: I receive the results of the DNA tests. With me are (left to right) Verónica Castelli of the group HIJOS and a member of the Hermanos Commission; Tatiana Sfligoy, the first grandchild recovered by the Grandmothers; and Estela Barnes de Carlotto, founding member and current president of the Grandmothers of the Plaza de Mayo.

December 19, 2007: Just after being sworn in as a deputy representing the province of Buenos Aires, flanked by Adela Segarra (center) and Adriana Puiggrós (right).

At the Campamento Latinoamericano of Youth for Change in Solidarity with Bolivia, November 2008, in The Chapare, Bolivia.

# Venceremos

Coast guard lieutenant Héctor Febrés worked as head of intelligence at the ESMA between 1977 and 1981, and was mainly in charge of what was known at the time as Section 4, which included various torture chambers along with the Sardá. Febrés was responsible for making the women write a letter to their families asking them to take care of their infant son or daughter until they were set free. Needless to say, the families never received these letters, just as none of the women who gave birth at the ESMA ever again saw the light of day. Once he removed their babies from the ESMA, Febrés was in charge of preparing the layettes and placing the children with new families, who had presumably put their names on a waiting list kept somewhere in the offices of the Naval Hospital. In his declaration during the trial of military officers in 1985, which he later sought to retract, he stated that he had tried to bring a more "humane" character to what was taking place at the ESMA. Perhaps that's why people who knew him said he paid from his own pocket for the clothes he dressed me in when he delivered me to Raúl and Graciela.

At the ESMA, the main officers always used noms de guerre based on animals: Jorge "Tigre" (the Tiger) Acosta (chief of operations), Alfredo "Cuervo" (the Crow) Astiz (head of intelligence), Rubén "Delfín" (the Dolphin) Chamorro (in charge of the grounds and proud director of the Sardá), Jorge "Puma" (the Puma) Perren (head of operation groups, i.e., the death squads). But Febrés's nickname was "Selva," or "the Jungle," because when he ran a torture session it was as if all the beasts of the jungle were let loose at once. Testimony from the handful of survivors recalls him as someone who was very tough with the *picana*, or electric cattle prod, which he particularly enjoyed. As a member of the Argentine Naval Prefecture, or coast guard, Febrés, who was also known as "Fat Daniel," functioned as a link between his forces and the navy itself, participating in or leading many of the operations carried out by the death squads.

After years of impunity and freedom that could only be construed as a gift from the government, the laws of Final Stop and Due Obedience that had allowed Febrés to get on with his life without unexpected stress were finally annulled by the Argentine Congress in 2003. Even so, it was four years before Febrés was tried and brought to justice. Despite the existence of the so-called mega-case of the ESMA, and despite the testimony of numerous witnesses who implicated him not so much in specific cases as in the overarching logistics of the entire torture operation and as a cruel, sadistic character with the power to decide on the life or death of the prisoners, Febrés was tried alone, and charged with only four cases where he had allegedly deprived his victims of their freedom and tortured them. Nothing to do with murder. Nothing to do with stealing babies. And after all those years of impunity, after the infinite comings and goings of

Argentine politics that had led the victims on never-ending paths from hope to despair, the human rights organizations and the plaintiffs had no choice but to see him brought to justice, even if only for four of the three hundred crimes that fill the pages of the brief against the ESMA. Once again, as they had done on so many occasions, Carlos Lorkipanidse, Josefa Prada de Oliveri, Alfredo Julio Margari, and Carlos Alberto García testified about the abuse and violence to which Febrés had subjected them, and about the pleasure and pronounced cruelty he took in torture sessions and acts almost impossible to imagine, as for example when, to make Lorkipanidse talk, he placed his newborn son on his chest before applying the electric cattle prod to his whole body.

But impunity seems to have no end in Argentina. On December 10, 2007, four days before his sentencing, Febrés, who had been comfortably imprisoned in a coast guard jail, was found dead. He had been mysteriously poisoned with cyanide. The sentence against him was never handed down, and the trial was suspended due to the impossibility of presenting the accused, who left this world without ever paying for his crimes. In this first trial of the military for crimes against humanity since the so-called laws of impunity had been annulled, punishment of the guilty, even if only for a minuscule portion of the crimes committed, had just run like sand through the victims' fingers. With Febrés's death we also lost the possibility of learning the whereabouts of approximately five hundred children who were either born during their mother's imprisonment, like me, or abducted with her. All the children of the disappeared who have been found, each of us with our separate stories, our suffering and our grief, still add up to less than one-fifth the total number of children missing from the years of the dictatorship or born during their parents' captivity. More than four hundred people, four hundred adults, continue without knowing who they really are or who their parents were, and without knowing their true roots. But like all the others, I'm living proof that the truth will come out sooner or later. Although the law of silence seems to have triumphed, the story is still not over. It has only just begun, and in the end there will be justice.

It is not my intention here to claim that there are different degrees of responsibility; that in the face of torture, privation of personal liberty, or murder, some people are less guilty than others. Everyone who took part in death centers such as the ESMA belongs behind bars, regardless of whether they were following orders or issuing them. Their different roles may determine the length of their punishment, but not their degree of responsibility. Still, the punishment a given crime deserves is one thing; it's quite another when it comes to the different ways the various people who paraded through my life are assimilated in my current life, which does depend on the role they played in my story and in the history of Argentina.

Out of all the characters who are part of my story, across the whole spectrum of guilt and innocence, there are two whose role was harmful and corrosive beyond the shadow of a doubt. One of them is Héctor Febrés, that fat man swollen with exaggerated self-confidence, the man who would jokingly call me "my little lefty" whenever he saw me with my ubiquitous Che beret. To think that I actually hugged him, that I called him uncle, that I thanked him for each and every one of the gifts he faithfully sent me every year on my birthday (a false, arbitrary date that he himself had invented), turns my stomach and unleashes a permanent, unending struggle within me not to hate myself. This sinister figure stood in front of my mother even before I was born, made her write a letter to my grandparents asking them to look after me, tore me from her arms only two weeks after she gave birth, and delivered me to one of his friends to be raised under another name and another identity, and without a past. Then, without the slightest remorse, as a witness to my false birth, he agreed to be my godfather, symbolically accepting that I would "lack for nothing." Nothing. His suspicious, frustrating death remains a symbol of the code of silence that still persists among the killers from the years of dictatorship. It is also a clear sign that those who decreed the life or death of thousands of people still wield sufficient power to continue doing so with total impunity.

But even more than the revulsion I feel toward a character such as Febrés is that which I feel toward a person with whom I share a tie that can be neither denied nor undone, because we're linked by blood. I'm speaking here of my uncle, my real one, my father's brother and the person responsible for the destruction of my family: Adolfo Donda Tigel. I find it unbearable to think that he was my father's idol and protector when they were young, that he was the godfather at my father's wedding to my mother, and that a few years later this same man was capable of sitting in his office at the ESMA while his sister-in-law—my mother—was being tortured in the room next door. When we're faced with someone so entirely evil, when the inconceivable nonetheless appears before our eyes, our only defense is to argue that this person isn't really human, that he can't be classified, that he has neither soul nor feelings. Yet I refuse to take that path: Adolfo Donda, my uncle, is a human being just as I am; the same blood runs in our veins. Precisely for this reason, he deserves the most severe punishment available, and every single one of his acts rules out any form of pardon. Hard as it may be to understand this degree of savagery, we know for a fact that he believed in what he did. According to testimony at trials and in newspapers (see, for example, Miguel Bonasso's article "La historia de Donda Tigel, el marino que mató a su cuñada y le robó a sus hijos" [The Story of Donda Tigel, the Sailor Who Killed His Sister-in-Law and Stole Her Children], *Página/12*, July 11, 2001), he bragged about what he was doing, and used the example of his role in torturing his sister-in-law to make other prisoners understand that his "mission" would stop at nothing, not even if his own family was involved.

Based on testimony at the trials, Adolfo Donda, as director of intelligence, was part of the group that met each Wednesday in the so-called Gold Room of the Officers' Mess at the ESMA to decide on the week's "transfers" and the murder of prisoners housed on the third floor of the building, right over their heads. After kidnapping his sister-in-law's newborn daughter, Adolfo Donda gave the approval for Cori to be injected with Sodium Penthothal, carried onto a plane of the Armed Forces, and thrown alive into La Plata River. For years, while my grandmother Leontina begged him, weeping, to do something to find her daughter, all he did was smile back and assure her there was nothing he could do, and that Cori was certainly dead. Adolfo Donda is also the person who sued my mother's family so he could adopt my older sister, changing her name and raising her with the lie that her parents had abandoned her. He is the person responsible for my parents' double disappearance: first, their physical disappearance at the hands of death squads directly under his command; and second, their symbolic one, which he achieved by destroying what my parents had left behind: my sister, by changing her name and lying to her, and me, by handing me over to a couple of strangers as one might offer a gift, or even a dog.

I wish I could have him seated across from me one day so I could look him straight in the eye and ask him what he did with my father and mother, and where their bodies are. Thanks to the ironies of life and the impunity still enjoyed by the torturers and killers of the military regime, Adolfo Donda is currently awaiting trial in a special navy jail under living conditions far better than those in an ordinary prison. Ironically, for years that jail housed the Naval Academy, the very same school where both he and his brother completed their secondary studies.

After I had discovered the truth about my past, I agreed to make a documentary that was supposed to be part of the process of "getting to know" my real family. As part of the project, I went to visit the Naval Academy with two former buddies of my father and we walked the grounds together. I eagerly soaked up the stories of their student days. When I learned that my uncle was locked up only feet away, I asked to see him. I wanted to stand in his presence like someone carrying out an exorcism by confronting his worst demons.

"Only relatives are authorized to visit the prisoners," the soldier on duty replied when I asked to see Adolfo Donda.

"I *am* a relative. My name is Victoria Donda, and I'm his niece."

The young soldier disappeared into the building, probably so one of his superiors could take responsibility for deciding on such an unexpected request.

We waited for several interminable minutes while all the butterflies in the world did somersaults in my stomach. What would I tell him? How to begin?

Finally, another soldier appeared, clearly of higher rank than the one who had first greeted us.

"Was it you who wanted to see Captain Donda Tigel?" he asked me, with a respect for my uncle that gave me goose bumps.

"Yes, I'm his niece," I replied.

"The captain doesn't want to see you. He says you're not his niece, because his brother never recognized you as his daughter."

I'm sure deep down I didn't really expect my uncle to receive me, and I knew he wouldn't want to speak with me, but that reference to my father was too much.

"Tell him that if his brother wasn't able to recognize me as his daughter it was because he never met me, because my mother gave birth to me at the ESMA, where my uncle had imprisoned her until he decided to kill her, just the way he killed his own brother," I said, holding back my tears and turning on my heels before that sad messenger could say a word.

To me, there is a clear difference between the legal responsibilities of the people who turned my life into a lie and how I feel toward their actions. I'm not trying to justify my feelings for Graciela and Raúl, nor do I want to excuse them for their role in this whole story; my feelings are my own, and there's nothing I can do to change them. But they are neither Febrés nor Donda, and the measuring stick I use to calculate that difference isn't hard to understand: it has to do with cruelty, intent, and cynicism. If there's anything worse than committing a crime, it's taking pleasure from it. And I'm sure that those two took great pleasure. The difference, whether it bothers people or not, is that I love Graciela and Raúl. It's not a love free of conflict, but it's love nonetheless.

But all of this would be revealed later. For now I was just starting law school, and in the process I was acquiring a political commitment that would be my pillar of strength in the darkest moments of my life, which, as it so happens, were just up ahead.

Everything seemed to be happening at a dizzying pace. Without even noticing, I was spending more and more time with Venceremos, and it was therefore growing harder to hide my activism from Raúl. It was the last year of Menem's presidency, and the former ease of the idle classes was a distant memory. It was then that the associations of retirees began their Wednesday protest marches in front of the Congress, demanding an increase in their pensions, which were completely out of sync with the economic reality of the country. In order to join my *compañeros* on these marches, which we attended in solidarity with the retirees and other groups on the left, my political mentor, Roberto, and I came up with a plan: first he'd come over to my house a few times so Raúl could meet him and put a face with the name I had begun to mention with increasing frequency. We would introduce him as my boyfriend, and once Raúl felt comfortable with Roberto we would move on to the next phase, saying that on Wednesdays, while our group was protesting with the pensioners in front of the Congress, we were going to the movies, like any young couple. Of course, when it comes to lying, especially to someone like Raúl who's so suspicious to begin with, we had to do things right and with professionalism. So every Wednesday morning I would flip through the arts section of *Clarín* to familiarize myself with the plot and characters of the movie we had selected on the off chance that Raúl might ask me what I thought about the film or, in a worst-case scenario, if it turned out that Raúl and Graciela had gone to see the same movie and wanted to talk about it. The strange part is that Roberto actually did become my boyfriend, and by the time it was no longer necessary to lie about my activism, we were actually going to the movies regularly, like everybody else.

In that first year when I was doing the Ciclo Básico and starting university, a girl arrived whose name signaled the importance that her friendship and unconditional support would have for me later on, when my life took such a sharp turn: her name was Victoria. And as so often happens with friendships that turn out solid as rock, where trust in each other and mutual affection are absolute, we took an immediate dislike to each other the first time we met.

In the eyes of my "family" or the girls from the popular clique at the Institute, I was a tramp, or as one might say, a slum girl. With my shredded pants, my skulls, and my scarves, I definitely stood out. As a leftover from my days in the rancid atmosphere of Sacred Heart, where I would do anything to get attention, I was always heavily made up and wore my hair long and loose, making sure my black waves were as voluminous as possible, and never once going out without my huge hoop earrings and high heels. Of course, what symbolized one thing in the world I lived in had an entirely different meaning in the context of political activism and within a group such as Venceremos: to my comrades, my painted lips, miniskirts, waved hair, and high heels were a textbook illustration of a *cheta*, a typical suburban girl from a bourgeois family. Since Vicky changed her hair color practically every week and dressed in a way that had led more than one elderly lady to cross the street to avoid her, our mutual aversion was, at first, complete. To top things off, while I seemed to grow more serious by the day about my political commitment, Vicky's mind seemed to be elsewhere, with little regard for our schedule and appointments.

What separated us to begin with was exactly what would make us inseparable friends in the end: while I was a kind of "army brat," Vicky's father was a *desaparecido*. She would tell anyone who would listen, in that tone that was so much her style and that made it impossible to tell if she was serious or joking, that she considered her father a hero: he had been a Montonero activist and worked, as it happened, as a nurse in the Hospital Durand, the institution that today houses the genetic archive of the disappeared. The "official" story for many years had it that a *patota* came to look for him one day, and that before they found him he had swallowed a capsule of cyanide to keep from falling into their hands and revealing information under torture. In those years, the national leadership of the Montoneros had distributed cyanide to all its cadres so they could commit suicide in case they were caught, and many escaped the military using this method. Vicky always believed that her father had sacrificed his life and gone to his death without "singing." But at a certain point, thanks to the testimony of survivors, it was revealed that, as in so many other cases, his abductors had managed to take the pill from his mouth, or pumped his stomach, and that he had wound up at the ESMA, from where he never emerged alive.

After recounting this last version, still in her customary ambiguous tone of voice, Vicky would say that when she heard it she was disappointed. She preferred to think that her father had died before they caught him. Today, as a kind of consolation for both of us and in an attempt to reconstruct the lives of our fathers, we like to think that my mother and her father were both at the ESMA at the same time, and that perhaps they even became friends before the first of them was "transferred." Perhaps her father even met me and knew my real name, the name my mother had chosen for me, and my name reminded him of his own daughter, making him want to see her again. Or maybe it was partly because of him that my mother chose that name for me and the two of them hoped that one day the two Victorias would meet and become friends. When we think this way, Vicky and I rejoice as we imagine that, in a certain way and entirely unconsciously, we've fulfilled their wishes.

Toward the end of the Ciclo Básico, the balancing act I had kept up between my political involvement and the lies I was telling at home about my Wednesday trips to the movies and my church work was becoming harder and harder to maintain. Encouraged by Raúl's growing resignation in the face of my ideas and by the fact that Roberto, my political handler, who was covering my back, had finally become my boyfriend, I did my best to keep up appearances because I was afraid of the showdown that I would sooner or later have to face. During that period I would get to the law school around 7:30 in the morning and generally stay until 11:00 at night. Once, when we were coordinating a huge gathering of leftist youth groups in the province of Córdoba, I made up a spiritual retreat with the fictional church. I can still remember how nervous I felt calling

Buenos Aires from a phone both in Córdoba to let my family know I was all right and that the retreat was wonderful. Behind me, just a few yards away, rows of different movements and political groups were marching down the avenue singing at the top of their lungs and throwing firecrackers.

"What's that noise in the background?" Raúl asked, intrigued.

"I don't know—some demonstration or something," I said, a cold sweat running down my spine while I watched my *compañeros* march, praying for something that would end our conversation. Some explosion at the phone company, an urgent matter on Raúl's side. Something, anything, before all my lies ate me up alive.

It was 1999, and the political climate in Argentina was at fever pitch. A presidential election was approaching, and the impact of the economic crisis was obvious across the board. Demonstrations, strikes, and protests were nearly constant. That was when protests became a part of the daily landscape as street blockades. Whether on side streets or avenues, the demonstrators, known as *piqueteros,* would announce the closing of certain streets for a certain number of hours. At the appointed moment, they would stand in the middle of the street and stop traffic for the amount of time they had stipulated, until they allowed buses and cars to move normally again. This kind of protest had a double advantage: on the one hand, it didn't take a lot of people to pull off, and therefore, on the other, it was easy to hold multiple blockades in different places at the same time, creating real traffic chaos and attracting maximum media attention.

With Menem launching his final, pathetic attempt to achieve yet another constitutional reform that would allow him to run again for president, and with the increasingly obscene concessions to international credit organizations, the active resistance grew more radical, especially among young people and the unemployed, who were now 20 percent of the working-age population. Patria Libre joined with other left-wing organizations, including my group, Venceremos, and the *piqueteros* movement, to form the Frente de Resistencia (United Resistance Front), with the goal of channeling popular discontent and offering a solid alternative to the neoliberal model of the preceding decade.

Finally, the inevitable happened. As usual at dinner time, we were all at the table watching the news on TV. When the national news came on, they showed footage of a new street blockade in downtown Buenos Aires that had ended in a clash with the police and with smashed windows in places like McDonald's and Walmart. Before my eyes, one of my *compañeros,* his face covered with a bandanna I had seen him wear so many times, hurled a stone at one of the windows. At that very moment, I felt a tiny chicken bone lodge in the roof of my mouth, and, as if it had triggered some latent mechanism, my mouth opened independently of me and all the pent-up words poured out at last.

"I'm involved with that group. That's where I spend my day, not in a church in La Boca," I said, without stopping to breathe, waiting for everything to collapse around me and everybody at the table to pounce on me like wild dogs.

But Clara had no idea what I was talking about, Graciela remained locked in one of her classic silences, and Raúl, his voice a mere thread, simply stared at me and asked, more out of fear than anger, "Quebracho?"

Quebracho was a revolutionary leftist group that admired Che Guevara and followed the ideology of the guerrillas of the 1970s, especially the ERP (Ejército Revolucionario del Pueblo), or People's Revolutionary Army. In actual fact, to a noninitiate, it was not very different from the group I was involved with, but with the media's complicity, they had achieved what might have seemed impossible: they had become the symbolic demon across the political spectrum. The middle class, the government, and the reactionary sector as a whole all saw Quebracho as responsible for the acts of provocation, the street blockades and the clashes with security forces. On the left, Quebracho was seen as the paradigm of an organization infiltrated to the hilt by members of the state intelligence agencies, who used it as a perverse means of social containment based on the concept that people would fear a "return to the past."

"No," I replied. "I'm with Patria Libre, the ones with the blue and white flag." I pointed to the TV screen. Taken by surprise at my own words, I began to explain the differences among the various leftist groups, which were not actually so great.

Although I could see on Raúl's face not merely the shadow of his disappointment but the confirmation of the doubts he had been harboring all along, the Manichaeism of Argentine politics saved me from a worse reaction on his part. Naturally, from that moment on, the ideological breach between us became unbridgeable. That's when I began to realize that my political beliefs were diametrically opposed to those of my family, primarily Raúl. Of course, I have to admit that to some extent my behavior was not very different from that of thousands of adolescents and youth who based their identity or their ideas on opposition to their families. So while Raúl continued to maintain to anyone who would listen that leftist groups were a cancer on the body of the state, or that the Armed Forces guaranteed the Christian values of the nation, I threw in my lot with those who believed it was possible to build an egalitarian country, and that in order to do so we had to confront the most reactionary sectors of Argentine society, the very ones Raúl believed were the "guarantors" of the nation's existence.

Today, however, through the prism of the truth that I was denied for so long, my view of things is very different. It's not that I believe we carry revolution in our blood, or that political beliefs can be inherited. But I do believe that my biological parents bequeathed me their character and way of being, their vision of reality and their need to do something to change it. This is where the weight of heredity makes itself felt. The character of my real parents has been in my blood from the beginning, and even though I was alone on the path that led Cori and El Cabo to their revolutionary commitment, the three of us share the same point of departure: our refusal to accept a reality we feel is deeply unjust. My parents' way of being led them to live as activists at a moment in history when the idea of the collective, of shared political work, hadn't yet been trampled by years of dictatorship and economic crisis. Today, at a time when individualism trumps solidarity, I feel that my mission is more than ever to continue the work that their deaths interrupted: to build a fair, collective society in which the good of the many always triumphs over the benefit to the individual. Along with many others, my parents sacrificed their lives for that dream, and I'm convinced that my obligation is to continue fighting so that, one day, it becomes reality.

While it's true that my family relationships, especially with Raúl, deteriorated from the moment I stopped lying to cover up my beliefs and my political activism, it would be unfair for me to say that there was ever a real clash between us, or that he ever took a stand against my decisions. In fact, not only did he not oppose me, there were even times when his support helped me get through complicated situations. Whether by bailing me out with a little bit of money so we could buy basic supplies for our workshops in the schools, by helping us round up chairs and tables so everyone could attend our meetings, or by accompanying me more than once to improbable locations where I had to be, Raúl always showed me that, despite the fact that we were poles apart ideologically, what mattered above all and would always matter was the love he felt for me. I value that and always will, even if the sense I have of his love is different today from what it was back then.

The only time I remember actually clashing openly with Raúl over politics (although it remains to be seen how much of what occurred had anything to do with politics) was in March 1999, during the official visit to Argentina of Prince Charles. In the context of a foreign policy approach that had led some to call our relationship with the United States a "love affair," and that had attempted to apply a grotesque, pathetic formula of "seduction" to resolve the Falklands conflict, the prince was making his first trip to Argentina since the war of 1982 had pitted our country and England against each other for control of the islands. Preparations were under way to receive him with all the pomp one would reserve for our most important ally rather than the representative of a country with whom we were still disputing the appropriation of part of our national territory. The spectacle our government put together for this diplomatic occasion provoked a wide array of reactions, from organizations of leftists and former soldiers who flatly rejected the presence of the representative of a usurping power, to groups of transvestites who felt their rights were being violated by a new code of "cohabitation" in the city of Buenos Aires.

To protest the princely visit, a coalition of various groups organized a march that would take us from the national Congress building to the Alvear Palace Hotel, in the heart of the prestigious neighborhood of Recoleta, where an unprecedented number of police had been deployed since early morning for the dinner arranged for the visiting Prince of Wales and President Menem. Fernanda, who had also become involved in Venceremos, was with us. I had had an exam that day, so I was more dressed up than usual, in a straight dark skirt and a white blouse. I also had my hair pulled back, which was extremely out of character for me. The group Quebracho was ahead of Venceremos and Patria Libre in the march, forming a kind of vanguard to protect us, as they always did, in case of any clash with the police. As we advanced along our route, we noticed that the police had started to fill the side streets, and we began to feel that we were entering a trap. That's exactly what it was.

By this point we were used to the fact that whenever leftist groups defied the government there would be a clash with police that would end in injuries and various arrests. That day, we realized the decision to block our demonstration and arrest the participants had been made ahead of time, and while the police were taking up their positions, lining up their water trucks, and organizing a force of forty civilians armed with clubs to mingle with the demonstrators, there was such tension in the air that the smallest spark was going to set everything in motion. Naturally, that spark arrived, although as can be expected in such cases, there are many versions of what happened and it's hard to tell which came first, the chicken or the egg. There was a sudden rain of stones and a volley of tear gas, followed by a hail of rubber bullets. Then, as we had anticipated, our escape routes were cut off. The row I was marching with had stopped before we reached the barricade in front of the Alvear, because we wanted to avoid a head-on clash, but it was too late. In a matter of seconds we were all running every which way like rats in a maze, each of us trying to save our own skin even though we knew it was impossible.

Because of the way I was dressed, which didn't immediately betray me as a demonstrator, I ducked into the first bar I saw and waited for the worst to pass. A few policemen came in to make sure no one had escaped their clutches, but I didn't look suspicious, despite my eyes, which were red from the tear gas, and my bloody hands. I had been so nervous that I cut my hands from tightly gripping the stones

I never got a chance to throw. I was one of the few that day who didn't wind up being arrested. Fernanda spent the night in jail along with dozens of others from the demonstration. When I got home that night, late and exhausted, Raúl was waiting up for me. The deep shadows under his eyes showed how worried he had been, especially after the media had fanned the flames all day with sensationalistic images of the events. When he saw me step into the entryway, disheveled, exhausted, and with traces of blood on my hands and clothes, he lost it. Not a word was exchanged between us. I didn't see his blow coming; I didn't even feel the pain. I was too tired and overwhelmed to feel anything. What I do remember perfectly is the slap of his palm against my cheek and how red his eyes were, with a mix of worry, fury, and the incredible relief of seeing that I was unharmed. That was the first and last time Raúl hit me. I suppose I understand: he still considered himself my father, so he acted like one. At the time, I believed he was my father too, so I accepted his outburst.

After that traumatic night of social upheaval and police brutality, Fernanda pulled back from her involvement in politics. Slowly but surely, we drifted apart to the point where we simply stopped seeing each other. Mariano, one of the people who had shaped my political awareness, and with whom I had gone to my first demonstrations, now moved away from me. I've never again seen the people with whom I spent my adolescence, who knew me as Analía. When my case became a media story and my past was revealed, Fernanda tried to contact me through the Grandmothers of the

Plaza de Mayo, but I wasn't ready yet to confront a period of my life that I had a hard time accepting. It was a time that, while not without conflicts, had been full of happiness, and that had shaped the person I would become, but from where I would have to rebuild my world after it had collapsed. Maybe one day I'll return her call and reconnect with her as Victoria. I have no doubt that the importance of Fernanda and all the others in my life is as enormous as the tenderness I felt and feel toward them. I hope the time will soon come when I can say this to their faces.

That last episode with Raúl marked the start of a deeper level of political commitment, and a break with the home I had lived in since I was a child. Meanwhile, although I had no way of knowing it, the Grandmothers of the Plaza de Mayo were launching a new investigation: they were trying to locate the daughter of María Hilda de Donda and José María Donda, a girl named Victoria.

The timer had been set on the bomb that would explode two years later. Analía's days were numbered.

# The Beginning
# of the End

In October 1999, after innumerable and ever more pathetic attempts to write himself a lifetime ticket as the head of state, which would have required a second constitutional reform, the ten-year presidency of Carlos Menem was coming to an end, leaving behind a 15 percent unemployment rate, a foreign debt of 150 billion dollars, short-term debt to the tune of 25 billion, and a public deficit of a billion. The electoral triumph of Fernando de la Rúa and Carlos "Chacho" Alvarez, who ran on a joint ticket, owed more to the voters' rejection of a decade of corruption, frivolity, and "Menemist partying" than to any real hope that the two conservative candidates would be able to manage a government that defined itself as left-centrist.

Thanks to the continuing financial crisis and the government's lack of interest in freeing itself from the belt-tightening measures imposed by the international monetary organizations, any hope of a turn to the left in Argentine politics was dashed before the new government's first year in office. As if they were incapable of cutting their ties to the status quo of the political class that had led the country during the preceding decade, it wasn't long before we again saw corrupt bureaucrats, votes being bought in order to assure the approval of laws considered "fundamental," and an economic policy whose only goal seemed to be that nothing should change. Toward the end of the year 2000, the more progressive wing, led by Alvarez, pulled out of the government, and a few months later Domingo Cavallo, the man who had been the leading ideologue of monetary policy under Menem, was appointed secretary of the treasury. The man who had invented the notion of convertibility, who had established the parity of the Argentine peso with the dollar, returned to power with all due pomp to mollify the terrified middle class and the all-powerful International Monetary Fund. But second chances are never good. What had once worked to soothe Argentines' eternal fear that their currency would be devalued now appeared more like a last futile gesture ahead of a defeat foretold.

Meanwhile, in advance of those same presidential elections of 1999, the Frente de Resistencia was joined by a group who called themselves Peronismo de la Resistencia (Peronists in Resistance), basically ex-Montoneros or Montonero sympathizers who disagreed with some of the premises of Quebracho, and a splinter group from the Communist Party. We received more than 66,000 votes, or 0.036 percent of the total, in the national election, but we had expanded our territorial base with a presence in most of the country, especially in the area around Buenos Aires.

Our task during the campaign was to cover the zone of the General Sarmiento rail line, which runs from downtown Buenos Aires to the town of Moreno. Whether by coincidence or not, this was the same area where, twenty years earlier, my mother had worked in the slums and squatter towns west of the city. It had been just outside the Morón train station that a death squad had kidnapped her along with a fellow militant, and where, in a square not far from the station, my father had found her shoe and had desperately shouted her name, firing his gun into the air. And it had been in the next station over, Ramos Mejía, that my grandmother Leontina fulfilled her daughter's final wish by handing a few coins to an itinerant musician so he would sing the Peruvian waltz "Hilda." Once again, although I couldn't know it at the time, I was following the same path as my mother, walking the same streets and involved in the same kind of political work.

After our sparse showing in the election and the first political actions of the new Alliance government, which confirmed that everything had changed so that nothing could change, Patria Libre and Venceremos continued our process of radicalization, and the ever-present media soon dubbed us the "hard left" (as opposed to the "soft left," whatever that was supposed to mean). This led us to deepen our territorial work. We wanted to broaden our base by winning over some of the traditional Peronist strongholds, where we knew that people were disillusioned by a decade of Menemism and the standstill represented by the Alliance. We used to descend on those barrios every weekend as if we were from Mars, peddling our magazine, *En Marcha,* from door to door. I can just imagine the dismay of the poor people who would wake up on Saturday mornings to find a bunch of post-adolescents in Che Guevara T-shirts on their door-steps trying to sell them political tracts and lecturing them on the class struggle, Latin Americanism, and emancipation. I can't help smiling when I think how innocent we were.

Still, there was no denying that Patria Libre was expanding as a political force at the national level, sharpened by a crisis that not only appeared nowhere near a solution but was growing by leaps and bounds, thanks to a government unable to rise to the challenge of much-needed change. We gradually realized that we needed to do more than approach people with mere propaganda, so we formed the Grupo de Estudiantes Solidarios (Students in Solidarity). From this base we engaged in various forms of community work, at-tempting to involve people in improving their own commu-nities from within. The first place we got actively involved in was Dock Sud, back along the southern border between the city of Buenos Aires and the province just outside it. Thanks to the support of a credit union in the neighborhood, we were given the use of a space where we could hold home-work clinics for children from the slum just four blocks away, where we would go to recruit them to a variety of activities, always offering some kind of snack that we would prepare with the help of local residents and bakeries. We also quickly got to know some of the Toba Indians who lived in the area. They had a highly organized community with its own cacique. It was he who suggested that we ask for a weekly contribution from local residents so we could buy fruit and vegetables wholesale in the Central Market and then distribute them equally to everyone. Every family that contributed two pesos and thirty centavos received enough fruit and vegetables to last a week.

This new approach, so different from our strictly political first efforts in the area, awakened a strong sense of solidarity, and we soon had a women's group who took on the task of purchasing the weekly groceries and who also helped by preparing fritters for the children. Today, so many years later, my mouth still waters when I remember the fritters prepared by a woman named Pascuala, a housewife with a heart as big as the rest of her body, who used to sprinkle them with caramelized sugar that left a heavenly aftertaste of honey in your mouth.

With the approach of the October 2001 legislative elections, which were widely seen as a referendum on the government of the Alliance, those of us in the movement began to consider our options. That was when we decided to make our first overture to the Peronist base organizations. Unhappy with the government's politics as usual, many progressives and longtime Peronists began to openly oppose the Alliance, forming new political parties and regrouping to carry out various political endeavors. One of them was the Polo Social (Social Pole), led by a priest named Farinello. His followers were based in the poor neighborhoods of greater Buenos Aires, especially in the traditional structure of sinecures that Peronist *punteros*, the equivalent of local caciques, had handed out throughout the province with the absolute power that allowed them to distribute various forms of "aid" from the national and local governments.

I'm still surprised when I look back at the different views

I've had of Peronism over the course of my life, even if they've tended to coincide with general public opinion: my memory of the 1989 election is quite vague, but I know I supported the campaign of the UCR candidate Eduardo Angeloz, who was defeated by Carlos Menem. Later, in high school, I let myself be swayed by the undeniable charisma of the president. But by his second term of office, when I had developed my own ideas and a deeper political awareness, like so many others, I equated Menem with Peronism. This is why, when we began to have heated internal debates about whether or not to join with Polo Social in the coming legislative elections, I was opposed. At the time, Peronism seemed to me to represent the dark side of the neoliberalism that had swept Argentina and Latin America, and the last thing I wanted was to be identified with political options of that kind. Of course, that was hardly the case with Father Farinello or with Polo Social, but I was incapable of seeing the difference. On the other hand, up until that point, my political activism had expressed itself within a relatively narrow structure; to me, an alliance with Peronism meant a quantitative leap into an organization whose members, however much we shared certain ideas, held views diametrically opposed to my own. I came close to quitting Patria Libre at that point, but Seba, a *compañero*, managed to convince me of the necessity of such an alliance, which has continued to bear fruit today in terms of enlarging the base of our party. In the elections of October 2001, Polo Social received five hundred thousand votes from across the country, winning them four seats in Congress.

No question about it, the year 2001 was a heavy one for Argentina. The newspapers were filled with articles on the continuing economic crisis, the reappearance of ghosts from the past, new and influential social movements, and widespread unhappiness among the population. On the other hand, faced with a corrupt, granitic legal system handcuffed by the dread laws of impunity and Menem's pardons, investigative television journalism began to proliferate, taking on the role that judges and prosecutors were either unwilling or unable to fulfill. There were plenty of sinister characters from the previous government with skeletons in their closets, and some of the investigations established frightening links between the mafia, the military, and the government. One of the figures who most stands out from that period is Alfredo Yabrán, who had become a millionaire overnight during the privatization of the postal service under Menem. Yabrán had ultimately been accused of killing a journalist and finally killed himself in 1998 under highly suspicious circumstances. But what could Alfredo Yabrán, the archetypal product of the "Menemist fiesta," have to do with me, my history, and my future?

The answer would come from Miriam Lewin, a journalist and former prisoner and *desaparecida* in the ESMA who hosted the investigative program *Telenoche Investiga*, on Channel 13. On the evening of November 21, 2001, she aired a program that was a tangential result of research that the journalist Miguel Bonasso was conducting for a biography of Yabrán. The title of that night's program was "The Silence of Two Men: An Argentine Story." Those two men were

Adolfo Donda Tigel and his brother, José María Laureano Donda. My uncle and my father. Without there being any way for me to know it at the time, and perhaps unwittingly delaying even further my moment of truth, the program spoke of the relationship between the two, of the adoption by the older brother of the younger brother's daughter, and of a second daughter who had disappeared, whose name was Victoria. They were talking about me.

During the program they interviewed a former Naval Academy classmate of both brothers, along with family members from Entre Ríos, and presented the fate of these two men so opposed by their ideas yet so united in a family relationship in which Adolfo was the best man at his brother's wedding. My father had been the idealist, the Peronist, the one who from the age of ten faced off against his older brother and would have given anything, even his life, for his beliefs. My uncle was a career military man, the one who followed orders with conviction and who had participated in the hard core of the ESMA, where he had held positions of responsibility and stood accused of, among other things, kidnapping the diplomat Elena Holmberg and abducting and killing her daughter, as well as my mother, his sister-in-law.

With the return of democracy, following his stint as the Argentine military attaché in Brazil and after avoiding punishment for his crimes thanks to the laws of Final Stop and Due Obedience, my uncle refashioned himself as the head of the "Pretorian guard" of Alfredo Yabrán, alongside other known thugs from the ESMA, such as Víctor Hugo "the Chicken" Dinamarca. For years he worked as part of the intelligence in Yabrán's close circle, hiding behind such fronts as the business Zapram, which controlled security at Ezeiza, the country's main international airport. The footage of my uncle, taken with a hidden camera, showed a self-satisfied man seated at his desk while boasting about being in charge of security for all the airlines that flew in and out of Ezeiza.

The program also delved into Adolfo Donda's past as a torturer, describing the half-smile that played across his face whenever he was torturing and how implacable he could be during the sessions in the "cabins" at the ESMA. I don't have the slightest doubt that that dry, cynical man convinced of his evangelizing mission must have hated his sister-in-law for her oppositional character, even in the worst moments. Nor do I doubt the hatred and mistrust that Cori must have felt toward him, which meant she didn't believe a word of what he told her when he said they would take her baby, me, to her mother, Leontina, for safekeeping until she was released from the ESMA. And she was right not to believe him.

By collecting an enormous amount of material from archival sources and conducting innumerable interviews, "The Silence of Two Men" touched on the adoption of my sister Eva, the threats to my mother's family, and the definitive exile they felt forced to choose when they left for Canada. There was also an appearance by someone who had played a fundamental role in their investigation, thanks to whom it became possible for me to retrieve my true identity: Lidia Vieyra, the then nineteen-year-old girl who helped my mother give birth, who was present when Cori decided to name me Victoria, and who helped her concoct the innocent plan to pierce my ears with blue thread. Beginning on the first day she was freed from the ESMA, Lidia had tirelessly looked for me, giving information to the Grandmothers of the Plaza de Mayo and never losing hope. But without meaning to do so, the Channel 13 program may have sent their search down a dead-end street by stating that Victoria, the daughter of María Hilda Pérez and José María Donda, lived in Entre Ríos, where she had been illegally adopted by a cousin of Adolfo Donda under the name Mariel Donda. That false clue set in motion a court case to uncover Mariel Donda's true identity, based on the facts that her birth certificate was forged and that she too had been born in 1977, and on the suspicious detail that her mother claimed to have given birth to her at the age of thirty-eight, when everyone in the town knew she was sterile.

In trials involving the restoration of someone's identity, DNA analysis is performed, and a comparison is made not only with the DNA of the presumed parents of the victim, but also with all the genetic samples in the database of the Hospital Durand, where the DNA of thousands of people who disappeared during the dictatorship is stored. Unfortunately, that database does not come close to containing the DNA of all the disappeared or even the majority of them, and despite the evidence that justified at least the initial questions about the identity of Mariel Donda, her DNA was not a match with my parents, and the case was closed. I can imagine how traumatic it must have been for Mariel first to find out that she wasn't the real daughter of her assumed parents and then not to be able to learn the identities of her biological parents or her true history. The policy of the Grandmothers of the Plaza de Mayo and other associations such as the HIJOS (Hijos por la Identidad y la Justicia, Contra el Olvido y el Silencio, or Children for Identity and Justice and Against Oblivion and Silence), the group that found me, is always the same: not to tell someone they believe to be the child of *desaparecidos* their presumed identity until there is a 99.99 percent chance of a definite match. Their aim is to find their grandchildren, not to provoke a second trauma in people who have already been through so much because of the dictatorship.

But this is how, long before I had any way of identifying myself with her, Victoria Donda was presented to society. And despite the fiasco, the Grandmothers of the Plaza de Mayo and HIJOS continued with their investigation, following other clues, always with the help of Lidia Vieyra.

Thanks to Lidia's invaluable testimony, the Grandmothers knew for a fact that Victoria was alive and living with a family that was hiding the truth from her. They knew that she had been born between July and September 1977, and that two weeks later Lieutenant Héctor Febrés had torn her from her mother's arms en route to an unknown destination. But they were soon able to add to Lidia's information an anonymous denunciation that confirmed their basic facts: the wife of a junior coast guard officer, who refused to give her name, had reported that in 1977, when she had just given birth to a son, Febrés arrived at her door one night with a baby girl in his arms. The child would not stop crying because she wouldn't accept a pacifier. She was a newborn, less than a month old, and she was wearing a particularly beautiful brand-new layette, like a little present in wrapping paper. Febrés had asked this woman to nurse the baby, and when she took the child to her breast she noticed something unusual: loops of blue thread adorned the baby's earlobes. That baby was me, on my last stop before reaching my final destination.

The circle began to close when the Hermanos commission, an offshoot group that arose from within the ranks of HIJOS, composed of children of the disappeared with brothers and sisters who were still missing, received an anonymous tip that called into question whether Raúl and Graciela were the legitimate parents of their children. For organizational reasons, I was never filled in on the source of that complaint, but the long and short of it is that a neighbor had found the "arrival" of a daughter in the home of an infertile couple suspicious, especially considering the nature of the times and Raúl's high military rank. The first thing the commission did was get in touch with the headquarters of the Grandmothers of the Plaza de Mayo to share and coordinate investigations. The number of denunciations Hermanos receives is minuscule compared with those that reach the Grandmothers, so in the face of two parallel investigations into the same set of facts it was decided that Hermanos would take the lead, coordinating their actions with the Grandmothers. The idea was to establish the identities of Raúl and Graciela, to investigate Raúl's role during the dictatorship, and to ascertain the validity of their daughter's birth certificate. Several of the forged certificates of babies born in the ESMA were registered by Dr. Magnacco, the same doctor who had signed mine.

Thus began a slow process in which every step was undertaken with the utmost caution, since the primary goal was to protect the person they presumed to be the daughter of *desaparecidos*—in other words, me.

Meanwhile, in tandem with the slow but continual deterioration of the political and economic situation of the country, my transition from student activist with Venceremos to a full-fledged neighborhood militant was not without its ups and downs as I was forced to learn a new modus operandi. Despite our endless electoral mishaps, it was as if our time as student activists had accustomed us to a certain status that we now had to leave behind. Venceremos was a solid association with branches in all the major departments of the university. Many other groups respected or even feared us, and in the midst of so much political ferment we could hardly help falling prey to a feeling of omnipotence.

But in community organizing, in neighborhoods where nothing happens without influence or favors, and where parallel power structures have been in place for decades, our role had to be rapidly redefined. Once, during the period when we were still hawking copies of *En Marcha* and trying to impose our political analysis, we set up a table with flyers and political readings near one of the train stations. A few minutes later, two threatening men came up to us. They looked as if they had just stepped from a movie about union mafias.

"Listen, girls, you better move your stuff from here, because this place belongs to us," they told Vicky and me, practically without even looking at us. "This spot belongs to the table from the General Confederation of Workers."

"Sorry." I interrupted him, unable as usual to think before I spoke. "We got here first, and I don't see any sign that says this place belongs to you."

"I'm not going to ask you twice," the same man said, while the other one seemed to gaze at a point on the horizon, right behind us, without saying a word.

"Do you have any idea who we are?" I asked rhetorically, and then I paused. "We're from Patria Libre, so you'd better not mess with us," I spat out, expecting to see fear in his eyes. But instead of fear there was ice and little patience.

"I have no fucking idea who you are," he said slowly, without blinking, "but if you don't get your table out of here, I'll move it myself along with you, your friend, and your flyers. Get it?"

It was clear that we were no longer in the courtyard of the university and that our rivals were not future lawyers from the middle or upper classes of the capital. This was a different world, one in which the tensions were solid and whatever terrain you had conquered you struggled to keep. In this world you had to fight for every inch of space. In silence and without looking at him I began to gather up the things on the table. While Vicky helped me, the two guys moved away but stopped about fifty yards from us to make sure we left.


As 2001 drew to a close, the social and economic tension in the country grew progressively worse. The international banking community, principally the International Monetary Fund, forced the government to keep public expenditures in the black in order to have access to future loans or renegotiate the terms of our existing debt. What this meant in terms of real politics was a further tightening within the framework of the same economic model as under Menem. From salary reductions for state employees, to a freeze on bank withdrawals, to taxes on checks and the threat of canceling year-end bonuses, the newspaper headlines only added to the general sense that President De la Rúa was incapable of dealing with a crisis that was growing more entrenched with each passing day.

Meanwhile, with an energy inversely proportional to that of the Argentine political class, civil society began to organize, posing an increasingly cohesive alternative to a country that was falling apart. The movements of the unemployed, the *piqueteros* or street blockaders, and other large demonstrations, in which we participated, were now part of everyday life. Union organizations such as the Central de Trabajadores de la Argentina (CTA), along with human rights groups and representatives of the country's main religions, joined together under the banner of the Frente Nacional Contra la Pobreza (National Anti-Poverty Front). When the government turned a deaf ear on their demands, they called for a national referendum to approve a plan with the motto "Not one poor household in Argentina." The measure was overwhelmingly approved: almost three million people voted for an economic plan that would guarantee basic unemployment insurance, with further coverage per child and for all those over sixty-five without a pension. With that victory, the Argentine people showed loud and clear that they were fed up with a political class that continued to negotiate new foreign loans in exchange for endless belt-tightening at home.

But the euphoria was short-lived. The final tally was announced on December 17, 2001, and only two days later the *cacerolazo* began—a popular revolt, fueled primarily by the freeze on bank withdrawals, that was put down by the police, leaving fifty dead and thousands wounded, and that led to the resignation first of Treasury Secretary Domingo Cavallo and then, the next day, of President De la Rúa. Over the next few months there were five presidents, the currency was downgraded to 25 percent of its original value, and dollar accounts were forcibly converted into pesos, with small and medium investors losing a lifetime of savings. Systems of barter sprang up, and Argentina would finally default on its loans and enter a period of complete isolation from the rest of the world.

In this roiling context, where each new day brought the threat of events with potentially permanent consequences for people's lives, the whole array of social movements, particularly those on the left, experienced unprecedented growth. Popular discontent and the need for radical change were crystallized in a slogan that swept the country like wildfire: "Out with all of them!"

On the night of December 1, 2001, I had gone with two *compañeras,* Laura and Lorena, to a meeting of the youth division of the CTA. We were dressed to the nines, because we were planning to go dancing afterward. We headed to the Plaza de Mayo for a rally, wearing the same clothes as the night before. But we were greeted by various motorized police squadrons, hydraulic trucks, smashed barriers, and bullets. Many bullets. We never made it to the Plaza, because we had to run for our lives, dodging blows from the police and inhaling tear gas. Lorena was completely nearsighted and had to take off her glasses because of the gas. Afraid she would run smack into a wall or into a policeman, I grabbed her by one hand and Laura grabbed the other, and the three of us ran on, dressed in dancing clothes, with masks to protect us from the gas, and surrounded by police on motorcycles. For a moment I thought we should pull the scarves off our faces so the cops wouldn't recognize us as demonstrators, but we had rubbed so much lemon juice on our faces to protect us from the tear gas that it wouldn't have made any difference, since our scent would have given us away. Worst of all, in the midst of all this chaos, my cell phone rang with the news that Roberto, my political handler for the southern zone and my boyfriend, had almost bled to death on the Pueyrredón Bridge, the main access route to Buenos Aires from the south. The mounted police had crushed him with their horses and torn the femoral artery of one of his legs. Roberto has always had this gift: if you were going to a demonstration where there was a chance of a clash with the police, or a risk of any kind, you just had to stand with Roberto to be sure that if something was going to happen it would happen to him. He was a magnet for disaster.

By January 2002, Patria Libre had grown exponentially, and our community organizing had borne fruit in the form of a new entity, which we called the Movimiento Barrios de Pie. This became the vehicle, and remains so today, for channeling people's discontent and their need to mobilize, to feel that there was something they could do as society continued to unravel all around them. There were new street closings and blockades every day, with *piqueteros* demanding jobs and food for the ever more numerous unemployed throughout the country. We would block the Pueyrredón Bridge, and there were almost daily clashes with the police. Once, on our way to a demonstration in the Plaza de Mayo, all the lights had been turned off when we reached the bridge. When we were halfway across, the lights suddenly switched on, and we were face-to-face with three divisions of police: infantry, motorized, and mounted. There was no way we could get through. Someone shouted that the old bridge was still open, and we all ran forward, the police on one side and demonstrators on the other. For a split second I was caught between the two, with a policeman staring me straight in the eye from a few feet away. The effect was like staring in the mirror: if I moved to the right, he moved to the right; if I moved to the left, he did the same. In the end I made a dash toward the back and disappeared into the line of march.

As the months passed, the sense of imminent disaster abated, though there was no letup between the police and the *piqueteros,* whom the media had now decided to blame for the chaos, instead of preceding governments or the IMF. After all, we were a more accessible target. The worst of these clashes took place on June 26, 2002, in what can only be termed a "hunt," when a gang of armed policemen, acting like the former *patotas*, or death squads, chased, cornered, and murdered two young workers, Darío Santillán and Maximiliano Kosteki, in cold blood. The brutality of repression is always commensurate with the strength of the resistance.


Barrios de Pie had organized itself in various areas—health, education, gender, youth, etcetera—and held workshops and an array of community activities under each, with the intent of creating a participatory structure from "below" that could resist the repression and inertia from "above." In the Avellaneda district we started a soup kitchen named after one of the founders of the Mothers of the Plaza de Mayo, Azucena Villaflor, who had disappeared under the dictatorship.

It was in that space, which paid homage to the same struggle my grandmother Leontina fought through the Grandmothers of the Plaza de Mayo, and where I worked believing all along that I was the daughter of a former military man whom I never suspected of the crimes committed during the dictatorship, that the parallel lines of investigation being pursued by the Hermanos commission and the Grandmothers finally converged for the first time.

Maria and Laura, two women disguised as sociology students, came by the Barrios de Pie workshop to take photographs of me for a research project. I suppose I must have wondered at some point why they needed photos for a class project, although I have to admit that it never entered my mind to question why they weren't recording their interview with me or why they seemed more interested in me than in the questions they were asking.

Later, María told me that when they developed the pictures and put them side by side with the photographs of Cori and El Cabo, there could be no doubt about my true identity. But the goal was to be prudent, not to take lightly the trauma and consequences such information could have for those they found. They understood that the main adversary in their search for the truth is the false compassion the average person expresses when they say that such a distressing revelation can only bring harm and destroys lives, placing kidnapped children in an untenable situation. Those who take such a position don't realize the importance of the truth, of how inconceivable it is for us to have to build our identity, our history, and our life without knowing who we really are and our true heritage.

And in my ignorance even I could not suspect that the event that would turn my life inside out had just occurred— or more exactly, the event that would shake my life to its very core. The month of October 2002 marked the beginning of the end on my personal calendar. If every end is a new beginning, that was when the conclusion of Analía's story began to be written.

But Analía was not condemned to disappear—I am Analía. What would vanish, or in fact come crashing down, were the structures that had supported her—her place of birth, her parents, even her true age. But Analía would live on in Victoria. Her essence would be redefined, but she would never stop being me.

There were still several months to go, and many events, before July 2003, when from one day to the next my father would go from innocent to guilty and would no longer be my father. When my real parents would be born and die in a single stroke, and the story of my real family would open before me.

But that moment had still not yet arrived. This was still only the beginning of the end.

# Victoria

Villa Inflamable is located in the southern part of Dock Sud, in the district of Avellaneda, province of Buenos Aires. The slum sits on some of the most contaminated land in Argentina: on one side is the petrochemical hub, established in 1914, which houses forty-two companies, twenty-five of which are considered high-risk; the other holds the CEAMSE, supposedly a recycling area, but in fact an open-air dump where both legal and illegal waste burns day and night. Hardly any of the twenty-five thousand people who live in Villa Inflamable have electricity or potable water. According to studies conducted by a Japanese research agency, the entire area presents a serious risk to human life, with heavy metals and toxic emissions producing high blood levels of lead, severe respiratory problems, and a greatly increased risk of developing cancer. The lavish 1993 opening celebration of the Shell coke plant, which had been dismantled in Holland after being deemed extremely toxic and then shipped to Argentina, where "everything is negotiable," was a perfect symbol of the no-man's-land that Villa Inflamable represented on the map of Argentine poverty.

Barrios de Pie decided to establish an ongoing community project in that godforsaken place that had been overlooked by both capitalism and human development, offering literacy classes and legal advice along with general solidarity work. This was where we came to know Don Vicente, an archetype of the sort of people one could meet there. Of indeterminate age, although clearly very, very old, Don Vicente had arrived in the 1990s from the province of El Chaco. With his white beard and flowing gray hair, he got by in a little wood-and-tin shack overlooking a lagoon of contaminated water filled with heavily contaminated industrial waste.

Don Vicente was an acquired name; he had a strange real name that I no longer remember, in part because he was illiterate and therefore we didn't write it down. Everyone in Villa Inflamable knew him just as Vicente, so that's what we called him. For months he was our most diligent student, arriving every day with his notebook and pencil, proud as could be to show us his progress from the night before. When he finally completed our literacy program, he and the other students in the class were invited to the Ministry of Education to receive a symbolic diploma certifying that they had learned to read and write. But on the day of the ceremony, as our little group was waiting to board the van that would take us to the ministry, Don Vicente was nowhere to be seen. Worried that our favorite student might miss the event, I offered to go look for him. When I arrived at his house, I almost didn't recognize him. He had shaved off his beard and cut his hair, and was dressed up in his Sunday best. He had even dyed his hair. At first I was taken aback, and very nearly reproached him for "falsifying" his image. But I realized that I had no right to judge him. Even though the event was an homage from a state that for decades had ignored him and to which he owed absolutely nothing, it was still an homage, undoubtedly the first and only one paid him in his life. They were going to award him a diploma, and he wanted to be more "presentable" than usual. How could I fail to understand that?

We encountered stories like Vicente's every day. To know these people, to show an interest in them, and to do something, however minimal, for them was what motivated us to return day after day and to keep fighting despite the obstacles, which invariably outnumbered our successes.

New presidential elections were finally held in April 2003, more than a year after De la Rúa's resignation and after five interim presidents. Since assuming the interim presidency and in the wake of the devaluation of the peso, Eduardo Duhalde had responded to the growing discontent of the marginalized sectors of society with more repression, culminating in the actions of June 26, 2002, and the deaths of Kosteki and Santillán. At the time, Duhalde's candidate was the future president Néstor Kirchner, but only by default, after his first two choices refused to run or were unable to obtain enough support. The other Peronist candidates were Adolfo Rodríguez Saá and the ever eager Carlos Menem, who had offered to run again as the savior of those who believe that the present is not a consequence of the past. From the terrible days of December 2001 and the intense popular ferment that had followed them, Patria Libre had fought to be part of a grassroots political alternative in

Argentina. That goal lay behind our decision to join Polo Social, and to continue our work on behalf of the unemployed and slum dwellers through Barrios de Pie. But in 2003, the election was in the hands of the Peronists, so we urged people to leave their ballots blank. I even remember a moment during the campaign when we wanted to paint our slogans on a wall in the street. We were standing in Avellaneda, across from two walls that were already plastered with posters for Rodriguez Saá on one and Kirchner on the other, both backed by the same mayor. We had only enough whitewash left to cover one of them. Kircher was so closely associated with Duhalde and the politics of continuation, and was also considered such a political lightweight, that we had no choice but to pick him. Besides, there was less of a chance that we'd run into his supporters than Rodriguez Saá's while we were in the middle of painting over his face.

On April 27 of that year, in his final sleight of hand, Carlos Menem won the election with barely 24 percent of the votes, and Kirchner trailed him with 22 percent. But, fearing a result that could benefit the far right (as had happened with Le Pen in France the year before), Menem decided to withdraw before the runoff and Kirchner assumed the presidency with only a fraction of the votes. When he turned to groups such as ours in hopes of consolidating his position, we gave the new president a list of points that we believed were critical for building a new model for the country.

In fact, many of our points soon began to bear fruit, or at least to be implemented, primarily those having to do with the crimes committed by the military under the dictatorship.

Annulling the laws of impunity, declaring Menem's pardons unconstitutional, establishing the Museum of Memory, and recognizing the work of the Grandmothers and the Mothers of the Plaza de Mayo were among the issues I considered indispensable for moving the country forward. And move it would. It would be shaken to its very foundations, until from deep within, whether buried in common graves or thrown into La Plata River, the truth rose up into the light of day.

And until, from so much shaking, it would deliver the jolt that would definitively change my life.

If Kirchner's presidency officially set in motion the mechanisms that would annul the laws of impunity, it's also true that the structure that upheld the protective cover they provided had been shaky for years. The path that led to overturning these laws was based on two separate points. First was the fact that the abuse and kidnapping of children was a crime that by definition had no statute of limitation. However, during the trials of the juntas in 1985, while some of the top military brass were convicted in such cases, the courts did not consider the theft of babies part of a systematic plan that was carried out by the de facto government. This meant that despite the judicial constraints imposed by the laws of Final Stop and Due Obedience, and despite the pardons granted those involved, the Grandmothers of the Plaza de Mayo were able to continue their investigations and to pursue various petitions for the restitution of identity. Despite our democratic governments' attempts to avoid "stirring up the recent past," the Grandmothers were also able to bring a case in 1996 on behalf of almost two hundred babies stolen

during the dictatorship by presenting it as a plan orchestrated from the highest levels of the military government,
which has so far led to the resentencing of the ex-dictator
General Jorge Rafael Videla (even if this time he was only
placed under house arrest due to his age).

The second point derives from the constitutional reform
of 1994, the same one that allowed the reelection of Carlos
Menem, the main guarantor of military impunity in Argentina.
That reform also established that any international treaty to
which Argentina was a signatory would automatically acquire
constitutional status, which placed it above laws emitted by the
national Congress. United Nations Declaration 291 on the non-
applicability of statutory limitations for war crimes and crimes
against humanity, to which Argentina was a party, created a
small opening through which, with enough political will, it was
possible to annul the laws of impunity that stood in the way
of bringing the criminals of the dictatorship to trial. This idea
gained traction in 1995, when the Supreme Court overturned a
judge's decision and extradited Erich Priebke, a Nazi war criminal, to Italy. Priebke stood accused of having masterminded the
massacre of the Ardeatine Caves in Rome, where thousands of
Jews died during World War II. The court's decision was based
on the same concept—the lack of statutory limits for crimes
against humanity—and on international agreements governing
the extradition of war criminals.

The only problem was that for an international agreement
to acquire full constitutional status, the titular president had
to sign it. Needless to say, neither Menem nor De la Rúa
signed the necessary document.

More time would have to pass before the laws of impunity could be annulled. The event that catalyzed the change took place in 2001, when Mexico agreed to extradite to Spain the torturer and murderer Ricardo Cavallo, known as "Sérpico," on the grounds that Argentina could not provide the necessary guarantees to bring him to trial. As had been the case with the Chilean dictator Augusto Pinochet, the arm of international justice was threatening to reach where national legal systems were unwilling to go. In a last, desperate attempt to protect military impunity, De la Rúa signed a decree that same year prohibiting the extradition of Argentine military personnel, based on the principle of territorial integrity.

Petitions to declare the laws of impunity unconstitutional had already been filed by Argentine judges in 2001, but the political will to take them to their logical conclusion did not yet exist. The balance tipped with the election of President Kirchner, who arrived in office with a new commitment to human rights. One of his first actions was to seek the annulment of the laws of impunity. But there is no action without an equal reaction, nor decisions without consequences. In my case, there would be no end of consequences.


The debacle began in July 2003, when the Spanish judge Baltasar Garzón reissued his extradition order for members of the Argentine military who had served under the juntas. The Argentine Congress was already considering measures to rescind the laws of Due Obedience and Final Stop, and was expected to vote in a matter of months, if not weeks. As a first step, and as a clear sign of the human rights policies his government intended to pursue, the new president had already nullified De la Rúa's 2001 decree barring the extradition of members of the Argentine military. This simple act set off a chain reaction that would end my life as I had known it.

On July 24, 2003, the Argentine judge who had received Garzón's petition, Rodolfo Canicoba Corral, ordered the preventive detention of the forty-nine men on Garzón's list. I was living at the time in a cultural center that we had established in a building that once housed the Banco Mayo, from where we continued our community organizing. July 24 fell on a Thursday that year, and, as we did every Thursday, the family gathered at the home of Raúl and Graciela. Our Thursday-night dinners had been a family tradition ever since I could remember.

I was surprised not to see Raúl when I arrived that evening. Graciela told me that he wasn't feeling well and that he was going to stay in bed. Raúl wasn't one to give in if he was indisposed; he would at least come downstairs to spend some time with his wife and daughters. We had always been a very close-knit family, and Thursdays and Sundays were the two days no one was allowed to skip. When I offered to take a cup of tea up to his room, I expected to see him lying in bed, looking really sick. What I found was very different.

Raúl was pacing back and forth, and was in the process of getting dressed. If there was one characteristic that defined him, it was the military precision of his manner of dressing, as if each movement had been meticulously planned in advance. As a little girl I had loved to watch him dress, always in the exact same order, repeating the same gestures as a result of all his years of practice. But that night he hesitated over his choice of shirt. He tried on two, and between each change he let out a deep sigh, as if exhausted by some super-human effort.

I was so surprised by this nervous, vacillating person who bore no resemblance to Raúl that I forgot all about the tea I had brought up and barely registered the fact that not only was he not sick but that he was getting ready to go out.

When he finally noticed me, he walked over to the dresser drawer where he kept his revolver and, without even saying hello, said, "Analía, I need you to stay here tonight."

I assented without a word and without questioning what was virtually an order. Normally I would have asked him why, or would have simply refused, because it would have struck me as an imposition. I would at least have asked where he was going. But that night I said nothing and simply agreed. I suppose I didn't ask him anything because I didn't want to hear the answers.

Raúl left the house at ten o'clock, still without any explanation, although he kissed all three of us good-bye. He had finally managed to get dressed, and, as usual, he looked impeccable. In fact, without being "all dressed up," he was particularly elegant that night. I chose to interpret his surprising sign of affection as a way of reassuring us about his mysterious departure. I remember thinking that his van had been stolen a month before and that perhaps his exit had something to do with that. Maybe a friend had found his van and he had to get it. I wanted to believe he was taking his gun as a precaution.

I sat in the living room watching TV. Normally I would have channel-surfed without watching any one program in particular, but that night I stuck with one movie and tuned out what was going on in the world. Even today, when I think back on that night, I can't recall the name of the film. For some reason, not being able to remember is a source of great pain, as if remembering the movie would give me the power to change the subsequent course of events.

The phone rang at one o'clock in the morning.

"Analía, it's me," Raúl said in a much graver voice than the one he had used with me a few hours before. "I need you to stay in the house a little longer. Call this number in one hour." He dictated a number that I wrote down like a robot, my gaze still focused on the television screen.

An hour later I dialed the number, unable to go to sleep or do anything except stay alert. From the way the phone rang, from the shiver that ran up and down my spine, and from the tone of Raul's voice in his previous call, I already knew that the news would not be good. When I heard some- one else's voice on the other end of the receiver, my worst fears were confirmed.

"Is that you, Analía? Your father's in the hospital. He just shot himself."

Raúl had attempted to commit suicide, shooting himself in the mouth with his regulation revolver. Perhaps he felt that he didn't have the strength or the will to face his past, to see the dead rise from their silent graves, and decided to spare his family all that would follow: prison, the stares of neighbors . . . and more. A lot more.

But he had failed. The bullet hadn't damaged his brain. He was in an induced coma in the Naval Hospital, in Buenos Aires. I had no time to cry. Graciela had always been in fragile health, which meant I had to take charge of everything. I went upstairs to wake my sister and her boyfriend, who had stayed over, and together we gently woke Graciela. I called a cab to take us to the hospital. Impulsively, I ran right into Raúl's room, not stopping to think of what awaited me: there was my father, whom I had seen a few hours before, unconscious and without a face. The bullet had completely disfigured him.

It was almost as if everything had been orchestrated from the start. The moment I left the room and walked toward the lounge, a television set airing the news told me what had happened. They were reporting on the extradition order. A list of names scrolled down the screen. Raúl's name was on it.

It wouldn't be long before his suicide attempt also made the news, stripping our family naked in the eyes of the whole country. When I finally understood why he had taken that tragic step, I no longer knew what to cry for: my father's suicide attempt and my mother's pain, or the reasons for his action. My father had suddenly ceased to be an innocent fruit-and-vegetable merchant from the Dock Sud market and had become one of the people for whose imprisonment I had been fighting for years. The images of Raúl helping me with money, donating the odd piece of used furniture to the groups I worked with, or simply driving me back and forth to places like the Azucena Villaflor Center were suddenly all the more incongruous, since Azucena Villaflor was one of the disappeared, kidnapped by one of the death squads during the dictatorship. The same squads to which Raúl, it now turned out, must have belonged.

Up until that moment I had managed to reconcile myself to being the daughter of an ex-military man, although that fact had caused a certain degree of friction with some of my acquaintances, such as my friend Vicky, whose parents were both *desaparecidos*. But for me, Raúl had always been separate from the dictatorship, like a loose electron who had simply put in several years of innocent service before becoming a civilian and a grocer. Now I was faced with the unbearable reality that someone I loved belonged to the enemy. This posed a moral dilemma that had no possible solution.

I was totally overwhelmed. Here I was forced to be the strong one alongside Graciela and my sister Clara, having learned with no prior warning that I was the daughter of a man accused under Spanish law of crimes for which, under Argentine law, he could not be punished. To make matters worse, he was in the hospital, unconscious, in critical condition, and therefore no longer the one I could turn to for help in finding a solution. In that wide sea of contradictory impressions, and with an abyss opening beneath my feet, there was no escape from what struck me right away as the inevitable and natural consequence of what was happening: I would have to cease all my political activity.

The three days after that fateful night are a blur in my memory, as if I had been swallowed by a cloud of doubts. But the worst was still to come.

Soon after Raúl's suicide attempt, tortured by the information I now had about my father, I could no longer stand the oppressive feeling. Finally giving way to tears, no longer able to contain my anguish, I decided to call the office of the Grandmothers of the Plaza de Mayo, with whom we had recently developed closer ties because of the government's newfound support for human rights. When I reached Estela de Carlotto, the organization's president, all I could do was stammer. I told her that I needed to apologize, because I had found out my father was a torturer, but that I also needed to hear that I still had the right to be politically active, that my genetic heredity did not automatically make me ineligible to keep fighting for the causes I believe in. Estela was understanding and maternal. She told me what I needed to hear, and struck me as surprisingly calm under the circumstances. What I didn't know was that Vicky, whom I had called first in search of friendship and consolation, had been a step ahead of me and had already called the Grandmothers, so that by the time I spoke with their president they had already held an urgent meeting to discuss my situation. Their investigation into my identity had proceeded with the utmost caution over a long period of time, and no one in the group was ready to throw all that careful work overboard, especially if there was any chance I could be harmed as a result.

Their meeting was attended by representatives of the Hermanos commission who were handling my case, the Grandmothers of the Plaza de Mayo, and Patria Libre, some of whom had already been in the loop for a while and were only waiting for the right moment to approach me. But things had speeded up, and they all agreed that perhaps it would be best to share their suspicions with me right away instead of letting me continue to believe that my father was a murderer.

Only three days later and less than a week after Raúl's suicide attempt, el Yuyo, a veteran activist and former political prisoner regarded as a father figure by the group, was waiting for me at the table of a neighborhood bar. He had called to say he needed to speak with me. "It's urgent," he had said, as if apologizing for disturbing me in such a difficult moment of my life. At least that's what I thought when I agreed to see him.

My memories of that meeting remain fragmentary. After leaving the bar, I no longer knew who I was. I felt incapable of processing all the information that had destroyed my life in the space of a few days. I do remember everyone's compassion, their desperate attempts to separate me from the fate of the man who had morphed into my abductor, and their extreme caution regarding the identity of the people they believed were my real parents. I returned home on automatic pilot, moving like a zombie, unable to bear the weight of what had happened. For a brief moment I was even tempted to end it all. I opened the drawer where Raúl kept his revolver and stared at it for a few minutes that seemed like eternity, while I tried to decide if I was capable of living the life that would now be mine. I hadn't finished digesting my father's true identity and his suicide attempt when as if by a sleight of hand he was no longer my father. At the same time I was incapable of opening a space to let in my true parents, since I was not yet being allowed to know who they were.

The worst of all this was the realization that finding out their identity was entirely up to me. Only a DNA test could determine if my genes matched any of the samples stored in the National Genetic Data Bank, but if I wanted to go that route I would first have to file a petition to recover my true identity. This might mean being responsible for putting not only Raúl, but possibly also Graciela, behind bars. I wasn't ready to do that. I didn't have the strength or courage. At least not then.

It's critically important to me to emphasize the support I received from everyone around me, each according to their role. Even Graciela, destroyed by a world that she had always refused to look squarely in the face, was perfectly clear with me: whatever I decided to do, she would stay by my side, even if that meant risking her own freedom. Also invaluable to me were the girls from the Hermanos commission: Vero, María, and Laura. Whenever I started to fall apart, whenever I needed to talk, to feel less alone, or simply to be silent in their company, they gave me their unconditional support, without ever insisting that I needed to get on with the process of recovering my identity. I have no doubt that August 3, 2003, after my double meetings with el Yuyo and then with the Grandmothers and the group from Hermanos, was the worst day of my life. I wanted to die, to disappear. For months after that, I lived in a kind of fog, surviving from day to day out of inertia and unable to make any real decisions. The worst consequence was stopping all my political involvement. It was impossible for me to work the way I had before, and I couldn't bear to look people in the eye who knew what I was going through. I've always maintained that it was my activism that enabled me to overcome what happened, but that moment hadn't yet arrived. For months I wore black every day, as if in permanent mourning, and all the colors in my closet stayed buried under my present reality. The most I managed to do was go out sometimes at night, trying to have a good time, pretending, if even only for a while, under the bright lights of bars and discos, that my life was the same as before. Throughout that period, Vicky never left my side. She even managed to find positive aspects in what was happening to me.

"Just think," she said with a forced smile. "Now we have something else in common: we're both the daughters of *desaparecidos*."

Neither of us knew then that we also shared a name. Much later, when we were both more relaxed, she would be able to joke that I had taken away her exclusive title to her name. "Couldn't you have come up with one of your own?"

There was a seemingly endless parade of days, then weeks, then months. Finally, eight months had passed since the "worst day of my life," and, while far from falling into place, things had at least recovered a veneer of continuity. Raúl emerged from three months of induced coma. Our conversations, his clarifications, and my comments will remain between the two of us until the day I die. He still has to answer in court for his role in the ESMA death squads and my abduction. But he answered all my questions and told me what I felt he owed me by way of explanation. The only thing I can add here is that he also told me, in his own way and using his own words, that he would always support me, no matter what I decided to do about the DNA analysis.

On March 24, 2004, I attended the long-awaited opening of the Museum of Memory. I had spent years fighting for this museum, and to make sure it was housed in a space as symbolic as the ESMA. The people alongside me in the struggle had spent much longer than I dreaming of such an important goal. Still, on that day, one of the most meaningful of my life, my mind was elsewhere. I had even considered not going to the inauguration. It was Vicky who made me go, choosing what she would wear if she were me and promising not to leave my side even for a minute.

One of the speakers at the museum opening was Juan Cabandié, and when he talked about his mother, about the criminals who had prevented him from ever knowing her, who had taken her life, I felt for a moment that all my efforts to hold myself together weren't going to be enough, and that if I relaxed a single muscle I would fall apart forever. It had been only two months since he learned his true identity, and the government had invited him to speak at this event. When he finished speaking, once he stepped down from the podium, I saw him turn away from the audience and weep. I went up to see him and put my hand on his shoulder.

"At least you know who your parents were," I said. "I don't even have that."

I knew that when my mother arrived at the ESMA she was pregnant and that, like Juan, I had probably been born in the Officers' Mess. I also suspected that the woman who had held me in her arms for a few days was probably the same one who had looked out at me from a photograph at HIJOS. Not long before, I had been at the HIJOS offices with Vero, flipping through the book of photographs of the disappeared, when one of the pictures caught my eye. It was a photo of Hilda Pérez, and suddenly, in that face, in that gaze, that mouth, I saw myself. I knew at that moment, or I felt I knew, that I was looking at my mother. My eyes filled with tears. There was only one way to find out: by doing the DNA test.

How could my mother have withstood torture, being pregnant in a concentration camp, seeing her daughter taken away, all for the sake of her beliefs, while I seemed to be incapable of making a decision that would cost me only a few drops of blood? I needed to see that all this had nothing to do with Raúl and Graciela or even with seeing justice served or judging those responsible for the dictatorship. It had to do with me, with my identity, with my past, and my possibility of having a future. I realized I could no longer wait. The time had come for me to do the test.

There are two physical places where the Grandmothers of the Plaza de Mayo have stored the genetic data of the disappeared: one is in the United States, in Texas, and the other is the Hospital Durand, in Buenos Aires. Two days after the inauguration of the museum, I went with Roberto, who after years of being my political mentor and boyfriend had become a dear friend, to perform the version of the test where the results would be sent from the United States. At that moment I thought the worst was over, that I had finally taken the step I needed to take. Unfortunately, things are not always as easy as they seem. The results never arrived.

Months went by. So I contacted the person who had been the main source of information in the failed investigation carried out by *Telenoche Investiga*: Lidia Vieyra, the woman who had been barely nineteen years old when she helped my mother give birth. Little by little, a kind of support group formed around me, with Vicky—the eternal Vicky—Paula and María from Hermanos, and Juan Cabandié. Lidia gradually became part of it as well. But I felt more lost with each passing day. My test results still hadn't arrived. I was tired of waiting. Finally I decided to redo the test at the Hospital Durand. I figured that one of the two samples would have to yield results. I just hoped they would come before I lost my mind.


I did my test at the Durand on June 26, 2004, three months after the first one we sent to Texas. That day everyone in my support group came, along with Horacio Pietragalla, another one of the found grandchildren. We met at the home of Graciela Daleo, whom I also have to call "Vicky," because that was her *nom de guerre* when she was a Montonero. I noticed that Lidia could not stop looking at me the whole time. She was clearly more nervous and on edge than I was, and in a strange way I found that reassuring.

"I don't know if you're Cori's daughter and I won't know until we have the test results," she said, on the verge of tears. "But what I do know is that the baby girl I held in my arms had the exact same eyes as you."

When it was time to leave for the hospital, I realized that I had forgotten all the documents. I couldn't believe it, but it was as if a higher power was working against me.

"Sorry, folks, but God must not want me to do this test," I said to everyone and no one, too embarrassed to look up while I continued burrowing through my pocketbook. "I didn't bring my papers."

"Don't you have anything?" someone asked. "Not even your ID?"

"I only have my Blockbuster card . . ."

I didn't know whether to cry or laugh.

Just as if I were in a movie, I felt the two Vickys put me in a cab and take me to my house in Quilmes, far away from where we were. I opened the door to my house like an automaton and asked my sister to get my papers. I got back in the car and we rode straight to the Hospital Durand, where the rest of the group was waiting.

Finally it was done. Now all I had to do was wait. Keep waiting, longer and longer, keep living between parentheses. I didn't know how much more I could take.

. . .

Between the time when I flipped through the book of disappeared and found the photograph of Cori and the moment when I finally received the results of my DNA test, Lidia Vieyra was not the only person I contacted who had something to do with the story of the brothers José María and Adolfo Donda. If Cori was really my mother, and if I was Victoria, then I had a sister who was once called Eva Daniela and was now just Daniela, who had been adopted and raised by my military uncle.

The first time I got in touch with her she agreed to meet me and suggested a McDonald's in downtown Buenos Aires. When we first met, I didn't see the features I expected. If I'm the spitting image of my mother, Daniela has the light eyes, blond hair, and lighter skin of the Dondas. From her body language and her clothes (not to mention the place she had suggested for our meeting), I knew instantly that we were two very different people: my loud clothes contrasted with her white blouse and tailored pants. Still, her mouth and nose were unmistakable. Exactly like mine. Exactly like Cori's.

"Look, I don't know if I'm your sister, but there's a strong possibility we have the same parents," I said, trying to break the ice.

"I don't care if you're my sister or not," she said without batting an eyelash. "I couldn't care less about my parents. I can't forgive them for becoming criminals instead of raising their daughter. Now that I have a child of my own, I don't know how they could have abandoned me."

All I remember thinking is that I hoped my test results would not turn out the way I had been expecting. There was no way that person and I could possibly be sisters.

"Look, they may or may not be my parents, but I want you to know that I'm also involved in a political group, like them, and I'm proud of what they did in their time, as I would too under such circumstances. So don't worry. I'm also a criminal," I said, standing up and leaving without looking back.

I hadn't gotten anywhere. I still didn't know who my parents were. The results never seemed to arrive, and, even worse, now I had lost my sister before even getting to know her. Daniela had been well indoctrinated. The long, sinister arm of Adolfo Donda Tigel had reached her. This would not be the last time Daniela and I were in touch. But our resentment and difference of opinions would forever condition our relationship. Perhaps one day we'll be able to build something new, but not for now.

I received the results from the Hospital Durand on October 8, 2004. The ones from Texas have yet to arrive. According to the National Genetic Data Bank, I have a 99.99 percent likelihood of being the daughter of María Hilda Pérez and José María Laureano Donda, the daughter of Cori and El Cabo. The first thing I did when I found out was call Daniela. I didn't want her to hear it first from the media.

"Fine," she said on the other end of the phone. "But for now I don't want to see you."

It had been two years since the day the girls from Hermanos first came to find me and a year since they told me that I was the daughter of *desaparecidos*. On that day, October 8, 2004, with a 99.99 percent chance of being right, I could finally shout to the four winds, "My name is Victoria."

# Blood Ties

I often have the following nightmare: I'm sitting in a chair in front of my bed, on which a tiny blond baby girl is crying inconsolably. She's crying because she's hungry, and my friends, who are all around me, beg me to feed her, because if I don't she's going to die. It's been three weeks since she ate. I tell them I have nothing to give her and that I don't want to feed her even though my breasts are full to bursting. I know this baby isn't mine, that I stole her. Taking a closer look, I realize she's the daughter of my sister, and that I took her away. Still, I don't want to feed her.

I have had regular nightmares since that turbulent year of 2003. I wake up constantly in the middle of the night, or I scream in my sleep, roll around fitfully, and sometimes cry. At first I told myself that if I was able to push the bad dreams away I'd finally be at peace. But things aren't that simple, or that easy. Today, I think of my nightmares and insomniac nights simply as collateral damage, the inevitable side effect of seeing the lines between doubt and certainty go up in smoke. Even now, in the recurrent dreams I have most often, I'm able to tell myself that they're just dreams. I play my preassigned role as if it were routine, as if I knew that no matter what, my life is elsewhere.

My life. The life of Victoria Donda, but also Analía's. Because they're one and the same. Both women are me. And to become Victoria was not simply a matter of administrative procedures and a degree of public exposure that I never could have imagined: to recover my identity was also to recover my parents' past, their families, their blood ties. And, therefore, my own.

Daniela was my first encounter with someone from "my" family, when it was still difficult and painful to use that possessive pronoun without quotation marks. It wasn't easy, and it was clearly not gratifying for either of us. From the time I called her to give her the results of my DNA test until now, we've been in contact only twice, although I have to give us credit for innovation: one of those times was by e-mail. I had already written her in 2006, asking her to please send me some things about my father, because the Grandmothers of the Plaza de Mayo didn't even have a photograph of him. I also mentioned the letter he had supposedly written to my grandmother Cuqui before they killed him, which I thought she must have. Her reply was terse: she didn't want any photo of her father appearing in a book on human rights.

Our second meeting in person, although not as casual an arrangement as the first time, was the direct result of the foregoing. Along with the photographs and mementos she was unwilling to give me, she was also refusing to share the financial compensation Argentina offers the children of the disappeared. Since money is the only basis for a legal request for restitution, I sued Daniela, my sister, to recover something as simple as a few photographs of my father and to be able to read with my own eyes the last words he wrote to his family. Of course, the basis for the trial is the compensation.

But that's the way the legal system operates. All I really want is to be able to imagine my father as I've been able to imagine my mother.

Much as one might wish everything would come up smelling like roses, my first contact with the life I had been denied was a resounding failure. It's strange, in a way, how different Daniela and I turned out, how intangible and almost nonexistent the connection between us is: our blood tie. Clara, my younger sister, or the younger sister of Analía, will always be much more my sister than Daniela could ever possibly become, or me to her. We didn't meet before our lives were brutally transformed, and I continue to wonder which of us got the shorter end of the stick. But just as I don't like to think of myself as a victim, because the word conjures up a sense of fragility with which I don't want to associate myself, I can't have pity for the person (Eva) Daniela, has become, nor be too understanding toward her, given what she projects about our birth parents and what differentiates her from me.

The fact is that even if I made an effort to delve into the traits we have in common, if I tried to forge even the most precarious link to her, there would always remain a huge gulf between us in terms of the way we see the person who played the most definitive role in both our lives: Adolfo Donda. To her, I suppose he will always be like her father. To me, he will always be the man behind my parents' murders.

If it was already terribly painful for me to accept my new condition and redefine the relationships that I had considered immutable, that first encounter with my "blood family" through Daniela was not exactly encouraging. But every family has two branches, and if my first step toward the Dondas was less than heartening, there was still the Pérez family to contact, Cori's family.

Once I had the results of my DNA test, I met with a second cousin who told me that most of my mother's family were living in Canada. Cori had been the oldest of four: two sisters and a brother survived her. The younger of the two sisters had been the first to leave for Toronto, impelled by financial considerations and the effects of the successive crises in Argentina. Her older sister had followed her in the early 1980s to escape the ghosts of her own history: first the blow of her pregnant sister's abduction and disappearance, and then the coup de grace of a torturous divorce and the loss of her own two children to her ex-husband. Their parents, my grandparents, finally joined them in 1986. Psychologically defeated by years of looking for their missing daughter and granddaughter, they were unable to withstand the aggression of my uncle Adolfo after his release from prison thanks to the laws of impunity. Shortly after he was freed, the former chief of intelligence at the ESMA sued them for custody of my sister, relying on the complicity of certain judges who still had a soft spot for the years of dictatorship and taking advantage of the growing conflict between the two grandmothers about how to raise the little girl. After winning his case and managing to change my sister's name, he wore my grandparents down with constant threats and pressures, so they decided to follow their surviving daughters to Canada. The last one to leave Argentina was my uncle, the only male, also defeated by the way his country had treated him throughout his life.

In my first days as Victoria, I didn't have the strength to open up to a whole new family, especially since I hadn't even begun to grapple with the new categories I would have to use to define those who had been my family up until then. Naturally I spoke by telephone with my grandmother Leontina, and from time to time I exchanged e-mails with one of my aunts. But I didn't feel ready yet to meet them, especially considering that we were separated not just by twenty-seven years of parallel lives but also by nearly five thousand miles.

As time went by I felt more and more incapable of facing the contradictions within me. I had to compartmentalize things just to survive, because dealing with it all at once would have been impossible. At first, my main goal was to reposition myself in the universe without regard to other people or relationships. This meant figuring out what it meant to be Victoria Donda, which also meant finding a place for Analía, whom I couldn't allow to disappear on the grounds that her whole life had been built on lies. For my sense of reality, I needed to keep more than I needed to discard, including, of course, my family, a word that required no quotation marks to conjure up a whole roster of people. Not just Graciela and Raúl, or Clara, but also uncles and aunts, grandparents, cousins. The fact of accepting and acknowledging my affection for them doesn't mean that, in order to be politically correct, I have to repudiate them as family. On the contrary, the process I've had to go through led me to broaden my definition of the word "family" to include aspects of both nature and nurture, and not let it be colored by value judgments that belong to other spheres. It was actually harder and more complicated to create a connection with those to whom I was linked only by blood than it was to reaffirm my affection for those I had always loved.

Whenever one of the missing grandchildren is identified, once a DNA test has confirmed a genetic match, the Grandmothers give him or her a kind of book that recounts the life of the biological parents, based on transcripts from interviews with people who knew them, family members, and their *compañeros* in political struggle. The pages I received gave me a deeper understanding of Cori's character, and the mismatched but adoring couple she formed with El Cabo. And in the force that inspired my parents, I recognized the same flame that inspired me, the same convictions about justice and our right to demand it.

My political beliefs had been my sustenance since the worst moments of 2003 and 2004. They formed a core that I considered true while everything around me was collapsing, not like a house of cards but like a heavy block of lies. It was difficult for me during that time to know who I was, or to value the things that had been important to me until then. But my political identity flowed from my personal conviction, from an ideology in which I fully believed. My convictions were among my most important pillars, not so much because they acquired an aura of truth that attaches to ideas but because they were mine, separate from the environment in which

Analía had "made" herself, and also because they were one of the things that most broadly defined me as a person.

As I flipped through the fragments of my parents' lives, once again it was our political beliefs that enabled me to feel so close to them. The anecdotes about Cori's character, her way of relating to people, and her insistence on opposing everything people tried to impose on her opened a new doorway through which I could see my own personality and behavior. And El Cabo's seriousness and firm political commitment, the respect with which those who had known him spoke of him, filled me with a pride that was almost enough to bring me back to life. Suddenly I felt completely different from the way I had felt two years before, when I saw Raúl's name on the list of those accused of crimes committed under the dictatorship.

For a while all I cared about was finding out more about my parents. Hard as it was to accept that the people I thought were my parents weren't who they said they were, it was even harder to have to take in two people who were only a memory, with not even a gravestone to their name and, in the case of my father, not even a photograph to turn to in my all too numerous moments of doubt.

But in the midst of taking my time to adjust to this reality, new information arrived that shook the whole fragile structure I was building: my grandmother Leontina's illness.

In the space of a few months, death settled into my life as an element impossible to ignore. My true parents were not only dead but *desaparecidos,* so I had no way of knowing how they had spent their final days, or how they had died. All I had of them were the pages in the book I had received, which contained only fragmentary anecdotes about their lives. Raúl too had grazed death, and with his suicide attempt both his name and he himself became grotesquely connected to other deaths, those of the people who had fallen into his hands at the ESMA. As for symbolic deaths, Graciela would certainly have to win first prize: her life had come undone, killing her internally. But these were not the only ones. Deaths were sprouting all around me like weeds, and it was as hard for me to control them as it was to control my reaction to them. In the process of assimilating my parents' lives, I was also taking in the story of my grandparents, both the Pérez family and the Dondas.

My paternal grandparents, Cuqui and Telmo, had both died long before I resurfaced—they had left this world without ever meeting their other granddaughter, Daniela's sister. I can't help wondering what they felt about their sons' fates. I know that Telmo never forgave his older son for what he believed to be his complicity in my father's disappearance, and I assume that Cuqui lived with a mother's resignation. Sadness and disappointment are powerful illnesses, and they were both eaten up alive until their bodies and souls had had enough. I wish there were a God, and I wish heaven existed, from where they could hug me and smile knowing that despite all the efforts of those responsible for my disappearance, their granddaughter had finally reappeared.

On my mother's side, my grandfather Armando, who had never recovered from the way his favorite daughter's life had played out, had surrendered to death only two months before I recovered my identity. His death meant the loss not just of the family patriarch but also of the man who had been a role model for Cori, the person who had taught her the responsibilities of an activist, even if in the end they disagreed ideologically over the armed struggle and resistance to the dictatorship. Armando was also the founder of a family tradition that continues with me: boxing. Cori, my uncle, and I continue that tradition, although when I began boxing I had no idea that my grandfather had taught it in his youth. I didn't even know that I had a grandfather who was a boxer.

So of my four grandparents, on both my paternal and maternal sides, who had suffered more than anyone the loss of their children and who had searched tirelessly for them despite pressure from within the family and outside it, the only one left was Leontina, one of the founders of the Grandmothers of the Plaza de Mayo. Despite such painful defeats as the loss of Daniela, she was probably the only one who never gave up the fight and never for a moment stopped believing that one day she would set eyes on me. We had spoken once on the phone, and I would occasionally hear about her through e-mails from my aunt Inés, but for the moment I had no intention of going any further. I had been through too much grief, too much change, too many bureaucratic procedures. Among the few things I felt sure of at that point was that I was emotionally incapable of meeting the people who had been looking for me for almost thirty years, listening to their comparisons and stories, and feeling their hatred toward the people who had been my parents and whom I wanted to continue to love, despite what many people said and despite my own misgivings. After all, I told myself, my real parents were dead. Why make all this effort to get to know someone who no longer existed?

But in March 2005, when I was working under Alicia Kirchner, sister of President Kirchner, in the Ministry of Social Development, I received the first of two blows that would lead me to change my opinion toward my new family. It may seem minor, but at the time nothing related to my biological parents was trivial to me: on March 24, after reading about a new commemoration of the 1976 coup d'état, my aunt Inés e-mailed me a scanned photograph of Cori. Up until then the only picture I had seen of her was the one from the Grandmothers' album. Despite its poor quality and the circumstances under which it was taken (by the same policeman who would later hold her in the station house of Castelar after she was kidnapped), it enabled me to recognize myself in her and to hope that if my parents were really *desaparecidos*, then the woman in the picture with the slight half-smile was my mother. It was as if I were looking at myself dressed up for a 1970s party. The nose, the forehead, the mouth . . . I saw myself in every one of Cori's features, and it became unbearable to continue looking at that set of pixels that stared back at me maternally through my computer. That second photograph of Cori reminded me how little I knew of my parents. The fact that Daniela was withholding access to their few remaining possessions while insisting that she would never forgive them for their actions made things that much harder.

I was an open wound, and it was much easier for me at that point to express my feelings than to hold them in; when I saw that photograph of my mother I couldn't help but cry—for her, for her fate, for myself, and for all consequences of which the unspeakable dictatorship was capable. While I was sobbing uncontrollably in the minuscule office bathroom, from the other side of the door a man's voice asked me if I was all right. It was Adrián Jaime, the husband of one of my girlfriends and someone I had known for more than ten years. Between tears, I showed him the picture of my mother. I would have liked to be able to say many things, to be capable of expressing everything that was making my whole body tremble, but all I managed to stammer was, "Isn't my mother beautiful?" In that split second, the idea for a project that would finally take me to my family took shape, but it was still too early. The second blow had yet to come.

It took only a few days. At the end of March I received another e-mail from Inés, giving me the results of Leontina's most recent visit to the doctor: my grandmother, the tireless campaigner and last survivor of my four grandparents, had just been diagnosed with Alzheimer's. What a terrible irony that after fighting for thirty years in defense of memory, she should fall victim to a disease that would erase everything she had lived through, even her sense of who she was. It was hard not to think that a merciful quilt would enfold her final years, wiping from her mind the immense traumas she had suffered in the course of her life. But at the same time, it was as if everything she had lived for—ever since, long ago, she had been separated forever from her daughter—were being cruelly taken from her.

My plans, such as they had ever been, gave way in the face of this undeniable reality. Coming just a few months after the death of my grandfather Armando, who hadn't lived to see me, and with my grandparents Cuqui and Telmo long dead, to lose Leontina's memory was to lose the last space in which I might retrieve the memory of my mother. When this news came, I was in the middle of the interminable legal procedures involved in changing my identity, which meant that the mere idea of traveling to Canada to meet my grandmother before it was too late seemed as far-fetched to me as spending Christmas with the Dondas.

The person who then appeared in my life is the man who now heads my political party and who I am convinced most resembles the man my father would have become if he hadn't been murdered: Roberto "Beto" Baigorria. Since it's been so much harder for me to reconstruct a sense of my father's character than it's been to grasp my mother's, and since most of his personal objects and photographs are in my sister's hands, the idealized image of him that I've been able to create in my mind has relied on the different traits of the people around me, people I admire. One of them is Beto Baigorria.

When Beto heard about this situation, he didn't hesitate for a moment in telling me what I should do.

"Don't worry, Vicky," he said (and "Vicky" still sounded strange in my ears at the time, as it did to the few people who had begun to use it). "I'm going to speak with Alicia, and we're going to try to get the ministry to cover your trip to Canada so you can meet your grandmother." I felt his heavy hand on my shoulder, reinforcing the paternal image I had already projected onto him.

"But I don't even have a passport," I said, resigned, looking at the floor and thinking that all I ever seemed to do was collect impossible situations. "I don't have a single document with my real name."

"Leave that to me," he said. "Start thinking about what you're going to pack."

And he made it happen. As if it were as simple as going to the corner to buy bread, or tying his shoelaces. While I was incapable of thinking, acting, or doing much of anything, Alicia Kirchner, Beto Baigorria, and many other people pulled together to make it possible for me to meet my family in Canada before my grandmother was swallowed up by the clouds of her illness. I will never be able to thank them enough.

But there were more than just administrative steps that had to be taken. The day I showed Jaime the photograph of Cori, when I broke down in tears, another project was born. I wouldn't go alone to Canada; Jaime would come with me. And so another *Victoria* was born, a documentary film that would follow me as I learned more about my parents, reclaimed the identity that had been stolen from me, and understood myself as belonging to another family with whom I shared true blood ties. This film was a very powerful and unnerving experience that took us further than I would have imagined possible when we began. The enormous difficulties we had to resolve in order to make it weren't just spiritual and material, but also political. I feared that, behind them all, still capable of violence even from the prison cell where he was locked up, stood the ghost of the man I would have to deal with one more time: Adolfo Donda Tigel.

Thanks to that trip to Toronto and to Jaime's documentary project, I've been able to construct an image of my parents that I think is sufficiently true to the reality of their lives. I became more and more convinced that my parents were mine, that their beliefs and political struggle reaffirmed my own path, and that if I had been deprived of the chance to know them while they were alive, no one could keep me from admiring them now that they were *desaparecidos*.

Jaime trailed me everywhere, and although at first I felt uncomfortable knowing that all my conversations were being recorded, the camera gradually grew so small that I was able to forget about it, or at least let it blend in with all the other objects and situations around me. The visit unfolded quite naturally, between conversations and memories that all had to do with my mother. Day by day, I came to know Cori as a person I could approach and in whom I easily recognized myself. I devoured with my eyes and hands all the letters, photos, and objects they showed me, even though there was more of the girl in them than the mother she was never allowed to be.

But not everything came up roses on that trip and not everyone, myself included, turns out the way we hope they'll be. I don't know what they expected of me, what features of their sister and daughter they hoped to see in me, but I suppose they must not have been completely satisfied, since I'm not Cori. I wasn't even raised by her. And the reverse is also true: Leontina had spent thirty years arm in arm with the Grandmothers of the Plaza de Mayo, fighting the dictatorship when no one else did, holding on to hope when everyone else seemed to have given up, but that doesn't give my grandmother a defined political credo, at least not one that agrees with mine. She was fighting for the return of her daughter and granddaughter, not for the liberation of the oppressed—at least not as her primary goal. But this is something I can say now in hindsight. At the beginning of my trip, all I wanted was to be able to tell my grandmother that I was fighting for the same things Cori had, and that we shared the same political ideology and activist calling. But my grandmother Leontina, exhausted from years of lost political struggles and crisscrossing the Plaza de Mayo so many times that all her shoes were worn out, raised her eyes and threw her arms up and, half laughing, half serious, as only old people can be, exclaimed, "God help us—another lefty in the family!"

I think it's too soon for me to draw any conclusions about what I felt during my first encounter with my maternal family, the only one we've had so far. Behind the members of every family there are actual people, and behind each of those people is a story of traumas, joys, and suffering that shape their personality across the years. I suppose that none of us—not my aunts and uncle, my grandmother, or myself—was genuinely willing to look at the people behind what we each represented to the family. One way or another, we each wanted to find Cori, or what we wanted of her, in the person across from us. I hope and suppose that in time each of us will find our place in this new relationship, but I know that I already took the step I was supposed to, and I think for the moment it's been enough for everyone. I returned from that trip to Canada with a symbolic weight on my shoulders, though I was also relieved that I had gotten a little closer to the elusive figure of my mother. The one who was most pleased with what happened in Toronto was my dear friend Jaime, who was already plotting how to continue our exploration, and in whose mind the documentary was already beginning to take shape.

My maternal family was not the only side we visited while making the film: we also traveled to Entre Ríos, where I met several cousins of my father's who helped me form a more nuanced portrait of the Dondas. We also went to a reunion dinner of former students from my father's class at the Naval Academy, who made me smile over and over with their stories of my father's high school political activism. By surrounding him with an aura of mystery and seriousness, they made it possible for me to forge more of an image of him despite Daniela's refusal to give me access to the things of his she has in her possession. I visited the installations of the old Naval Academy, now a prison where, irony of ironies, my uncle Adolfo Donda is locked up. I've already written of that visit, and how I was suddenly convinced that the only way I would really know my parents would be if I spoke face-to-face with my uncle, probably the only person on earth, now that Febrés was dead, who could tell me how they spent their final months. But I haven't mentioned the consequences of that day.

I will never fully understand whether what happened was in direct response to our documentary. I figure that Adolfo must have looked into the film Jaime was making about me. With the military attitude that says first shoot, then ask, he may have mobilized things from inside the prison to make sure that, once again, nothing of my story and the role he had played in it was made public.

One day, a group of armed men broke into Jaime's production studio and stole everything they could get their hands on, tying up everyone who was unfortunate to be there at the time. The offices of the Grandmothers and HIJOS received not only letters but also phone threats to halt the project. In my own house, I even found a note telling me to shut up, which as if by some creepy twist in time was signed by the Triple A and accompanied by a cute little bow tied with a blue ribbon. Minutes after I phoned the Grandmothers to discuss how we could join forces to defend ourselves, my phone rang. When I picked up, I heard a tape recording of the conversation I had just finished having with Estela de Carlotto.

An endless number of things happened during the filming of *Victoria*, many of which are reflected in the way the film was edited, with scenes that show my story stripped bare, and with it, the story of a country that still has problems acknowledging and accepting its past. It's not my intent here to relate a series of anecdotes, but I do want to evoke one other moment in the filming that illustrates the tangled feelings constantly stirred up by the waves of memory. It was while we were interviewing Lidia Vieyra, whose hand I held as we walked for the first time down the hallways of the Officers' Mess at the ESMA, while she showed me the places she had been confined with my mother while they were both imprisoned there. I remember the shivers and tears that overcame me when, pointing to a tiny room that measured barely six feet square, she said it was the famous Sardà, the room where I was born. It was here that Cori had named me Victoria and where, in her innocence and desperation, she had believed that two little threads in my ears would let me have a life when it seemed I was destined to have none. When I couldn't bear to stay another second in that place of death and destruction and asked for the cameras to stop filming, Lidia grabbed me by the arm and, with tears in her eyes, whispered in my ear, "This time no one's going to prevent the two of us from leaving."

Despite the threats, the hardships, and the setbacks, the documentary *Victoria* finally had its premiere, and although it may sound trivial, for me it was a small triumph in the face of those same forces who shield themselves in impunity and shadow, continuing to believe that violence and illegality will make them invincible.

This is how, cobbling things together, going back and forth over the past and still with a long road to hoe before me, I gradually reconstructed not only the figures of my mother and father, Cori and El Cabo, but also the blood ties that had been hidden for the first twenty-seven years of my life. The process is as painful as it is long, and its greatest challenge lies not in seizing the truth but in discovering a new way of loving everybody else, and of finding the points we have in common that allow me to bring them all together in what has become a totally new life. I know that for me there will always be a difficult yet blurry line between the idea of family determined by ties of blood and this other family, the one I always considered my own. Despite my history, the feelings I have toward them are no less close, but they have an obligation to analyze their respective layers of responsibility and guilt. I'm perfectly aware that for someone standing outside my life, it may be difficult to accept and understand the relationship I still maintain with them.

No one is exempt from feeling, and we can't always justify our feelings only through the implacable logic of emotion. This is why, despite the lies, the truth I laid bare, the crimes and the complicity, and the roles each of them played throughout my life, my family continues to be mine, and can't be defined only by my blood ties. Clara will always be my sister even if our DNA tests disprove that, and my relationship with her will always be more like a sibling's than whatever I eventually manage to establish with Daniela, with whom my only link is our heredity.

It's Clara's turn now to be going through a difficult period in her life, and it will be up to her, as it was to me, to choose her own pace for contacting her blood family and reestablishing her connection with the family she thought was hers. I understand her pain as only someone who has been through this can understand it. This is where our ties are reaffirmed, where no test can destroy relationships created over years of sharing the same life.

Clara knows she can always count on me. I will always be her big sister.

# Public and Private

The line that day at the National Registry of Vital Records on Azopardo Street seemed infinite. I whiled away the time by listening to music, since I knew I wouldn't be able to concentrate on reading, even if it was just the morning paper. After three months of never-ending bureaucratic steps and legal proceedings that were a textbook illustration of what's meant by "the slow wheels of justice," I had finally decided to change all my identity documents to match my new birth certificate, which bore the name to which I was still not fully accustomed. At last I reached one of the glass windows, where a heavily made-up middle-aged woman struggled in vain to understand what I was asking for.

"But were you born in Argentina or abroad?" she asked without looking at me, protected by her gigantic bright vermillion fingernails.

"In Argentina. I'm Argentine," I replied, determined to provide no further explanation.

"Then why didn't you ever get your national ID?"

I had spent months explaining my situation to friends, acquaintances, government employees, and others, slowly getting used to being called Victoria, and I was tired. Tired of feeling that I had to keep justifying my existence, tired of feeling like a Martian.

"Please," I said with what I thought was contained rage, but which was obviously transparent. "All I need you to do is apply this court order and give me the ID. Everything else is irrelevant."

"Yes, of course," she said, as if she understood, again without looking at me once. "Just one moment . . ."

She disappeared behind a door and reappeared five minutes later accompanied by another woman, this one older and more worn down. I assumed this was her superior, so I repeated my whole speech, again determined not to give any unnecessary explanations. But this conversation was no different from the first one. It was clear neither of these women would lift a finger until they understood every last detail of who I was. When a third woman appeared, still older and still more beat up than either of the two previous ones, and began to ask me the same questions, I blew up.

I had always defined myself as a fairly tough woman, both as an activist and in my private life. Tears had always struck me as a sign of weakness, and I never cried in public. But so many things had happened to me in a short period of time, and the changes had been so brutal, that in less than a year I had cried more than in all the preceding years of my life. Confronted with my sudden tears of frustration and exhaustion, those three women did what any administrative employee would do when faced with an insoluble problem: call their superior, especially if it was a man.

Seated on a chair in the office of the director of the National Registry of Vital Records, I tried once more to explain what I needed, resigned by now to offering more details than I would have liked. Before me on the table, the director had placed a piece of Toblerone chocolate and a glass of water, with the hope of calming my agitated nerves. Finally, exasperated by trying to resolve a problem that surpassed his understanding, and having to deal with a girl who was intent on not clearing up his questions, he signed the authorization for me to receive an identity document with the next serial number in line, even though it didn't correspond to my date of birth. In other words, although my birth certificate showed that I was born in 1979, my newly issued ID begins with 18,000,000, as if I were forty years old. When I finally headed toward the door clutching my new document, with red, swollen eyes and a tear-streaked face, I noticed a young man on line still waiting to get in. He was barely holding back tears, and I recognized the same frustration on his face as on mine. We hugged like two people who meet in a desert of despair. It was Pablo Moyano, a grandchild recovered by the Grandmothers of the Plaza de Mayo in 1983, when he was only seven years old. Twenty-two years after recovering his identity, he seemed to be in a situation no different from my own.

I left that building I had come to hate resigned to the knowledge that this was a situation I was condemned to repeat throughout my life. No public administration is prepared to hand a new identity to someone who has lived for years with another. Not even the administration of a country responsible for that very situation.

The story of my national identity card was just the latest drop in a glass that seems to be constantly on the verge of overflowing but which probably never will. I still haven't resolved the problem of my name at the law school, where I owe a few more credits; the necessary change is tied up in red tape. The same thing happened with my social security number. In order to work, pay taxes, and contribute to my pension, I first had to cancel out the old number and be issued a new one. The result: two numbers, and the loss of all my prior contributions because I changed identities. If obtaining a passport wasn't yet another tangled story, it's because Beto Baigorria handled all the arrangements for me to go to Canada. These may seem like mere details, but the fact is that each of these events seeped into my daily life, siphoning off strength and making that difficult time in my life an even more uphill struggle than it needed to be.

The Grandmothers of the Plaza de Mayo don't work only to track down their missing grandchildren; over the years, they've also managed to construct a support network composed of their own members, other young people who've already been through the same experience, and psychologists who accompany the newly found person from the very first day. Thanks to all of them, from the very beginning I felt that I would never be alone. The support of other grandchildren, such as Juan Cabandié and Manuel Gonçalves, was critical to me, not just because they had been through similar situations but because by virtue of that experience they knew what it was like to become public figures from one day to the next. Even Paula, from HIJOS, had spelled it out for me in black and white: so long as I wasn't comfortable with it, no one was going to force me to make public appearances or make declarations to the media.

As for the network of psychologists, while it is certainly top-notch, I prefer to say simply, like so many others, that it's just not for me. And not for lack of trying: the process of integrating a new identity into my life was long and painful, and at no point did I think I could go it alone. The first professional I saw was a woman, but from the very first moment I felt that we were incompatible. I don't want to go into the details, because I'm sure it had much more to do with resistance on my part than with anything concrete, but there was no chemistry between us. After trying a couple of times, I decided not to go back to her. Shortly afterward there was another attempt, this time with a man. I went for a few sessions, which at least helped me to set priorities, and then I stopped going. But I was becoming an increasingly notorious person, and when I was included on the list of candidates to represent the province of Buenos Aires in Congress, even friends within the movement began suggesting that I see a psychologist. They felt that my level of exposure forced me to keep retelling my story, and that I was going to need professional help to process it. I began to go again, although this time around I was almost under an armed guard. My boyfriend, who was also my political mentor, would wake me up every morning and escort me to the psychologist's office and then wait for me in the square across the street or in the café on the corner so he could then walk me home. It didn't take me long to rebel again. I hadn't come all this way to be hovered over as if I needed a babysitter. I had always been the strong one, the one who was always prepared. This was hardly the time for me to change.

I discussed this requirement further with Humberto Tumini, founder of the Corriente Patria Libre, cofounder of the Movimiento Libres del Sur, a great *compañero*, and one of the people I've most admired in my life. Our conversation was tragicomic. He laid out his arguments with the calm and patience of a father. It was no longer just about me but about all the people I would represent, both within the movement and outside it. I needed to be focused, and I couldn't allow myself to move in a direction that I was unsure of being able to withstand. I told him that I was determined to be treated like an adult capable of making my own decisions and taking responsibility for the consequences of my actions. For as long as I live I'll remember the two of us sitting in his office while he made me solemnly swear that I would go to therapy, and I promised him I would, but only for three months.

After those three months, I stopped going. That's not to say I'll never find myself in that situation again, because I don't want to believe that psychoanalysis is not for me. And I have to say that Darío, the second shrink I saw, became a real friend. Maybe it's just a matter of timing, and one day I'll know how to take advantage of this form of introspection. Meanwhile, my nightmares continue with horrific frequency and have become a routine part of my everyday life. Night after night, my unconscious shouts at me with traumatic metaphors I seem incapable of assimilating, and day after day when I wake up I find myself expressing the same hope: to once again feel "normal."

The passage into public life is a lot like the sensation the fairy-tale emperor must have felt when he found himself parading down the street stark naked. There's no need to delve into personal matters to see what people might find interesting or stop to consider what you might or might not want to reveal. That's what journalists are for. As if they had access to an inexhaustible fountain of revelations, they've reconstructed every aspect of my story, obtaining information from the most inconceivable sources or, in many cases, inventing what they needed to fill in the gaps.

From the moment this chapter of my life began, which is to say from the moment my name appeared in public as grandchild number 78 found by the Grandmothers of the Plaza de Mayo, I knew that sooner or later I would have to deal with the media, unless I decided to abandon my career as a political activist and doom myself to be ostracized. At first it was extremely hard, since every time the theme came up my eyes would fill with tears. For most of the first two years after October 2004, I was incapable of holding back my grief. The nightmares, the failed attempts at therapy, the endless trips to and from bureaucratic offices were more than enough for me. But then, little by little, I understood that the best exorcism takes place through words. The best way to banish one's ghosts is to confront them, and there are few more efficient ways to do that than by exposing them to the light of day. When I first agreed to be interviewed and make public appearances, I proceeded gradually and with caution; and that's what enabled me to free myself from the enormous weight of my new life. It turned out that telling my story over and over enabled me to process things differently, to make decisions, and above all to stop crying. I had always considered myself a strong person, but that had changed, and I no longer recognized myself in the woman who would collapse in tears of anguish at the slightest mention of the fact that she was the daughter of *desaparecidos*. I had spent two years crying. That was enough. It was time to pick up the reins again.

Meanwhile, ever since the elections of 2003, in which he had won a pyrrhic victory, the government of Néstor Kirchner had expressed clear support for human rights, had resumed the trials of the former military by annulling the laws of impunity, and was pursuing negotiations with its foreign lenders in order to reverse the default into which Argentina had fallen in early 2002. In 2004, Libres del Sur, a new political movement we created by broadening the bases of Patria Libre, joined the government when several of our members were appointed to key positions in the administration, especially in human rights and the Ministry of Social Development.

That was the year when I began to work with Secretary Alicia Kirchner, and when I traveled to Canada to meet my grandmother and other members of my mother's family. I was involved in the National Department for Youth and the Program of Community Organizers for Social Change. In the Ministry for Social Development we created one of the programs I'm proudest of to this day: the Project for the Dissemination and Promotion of Human Rights, to which we gave the name Claudia Falcone in homage to one of the teenagers who disappeared during the dictatorship on the so-called Night of the Pencils. Thanks to this project, with which I continue to be involved, I had the opportunity to travel the country to work with young people on activities that preserve our recent historical memory and that allow them to reflect on the role of human rights in their country and throughout the world, and to analyze the different moments in history when human rights were recognized in the universal declarations of the United Nations. My experience in the Claudia Falcone project wasn't just politically enriching, it was also important to me on a personal level. For a long time I had been feeling uncomfortable and lost, as if I were moving forward without a direction, letting myself be carried along by impulses that were often more self-destructive than constructive. Once again I began a relationship with the man who was my political higher-up and who remained in charge of the Claudia Falcone project when I left the ministry. He helped me recover my lost stability and at least a part of my self-esteem, and played a crucial role in my leap into elective office, which led to my becoming a national representative in 2007. We're still together today, and although I can't do him full justice in this book, I would like these lines at least to mention the central place he's held in my life in the years since 2004.

And so we arrived at the elections of 2005, in which the government played a very important card: as President Kirchner had previously won with only 22 percent of the vote and avoided a runoff, these next elections would define his true base of support. I was working at the time primarily in the province of Buenos Aires, and my home was in the district of Avellaneda, in the southern part of the area outside the city. In part because of the female quota (by law at least 30 percent of candidates must be women), in part because I was officially living in the province of Buenos Aires, and a little bit, I hope, because of my accomplishments during the years I'd been working in the area, I was nominated as a candidate to the City Council of Avellaneda, as the sixth name on the slate. Naturally, only five were chosen. Still, due to a reshuffling of the lists after the election, my name rose to the rank of substitute, and I began my first legislative experience. This was when we launched the first projects in defense of human rights, job training and employment programs for local youth, and a legislative struggle for gender equity. From this experience I gradually developed the profile that would define me as a candidate when I decided to run for Congress later on.

Meanwhile, I was gradually moving toward a decision that was inexorably taking shape, although just thinking about it gives me a terrible feeling of emptiness. I was still working for the Claudia Falcone project and the Ministry for Social Development, where I was responsible for Youth in the Movement, although I was also spending a lot of time on my legislative duties. Sooner or later I knew that I would have to define the political path I planned to follow, and that this meant leaving behind the very thing that had inspired me to enter politics in the first place: community organizing, and working with people in the barrios. Unfortunately, it's impossible to be in both places at once. The joy and satisfaction I derived from my legislative work were overshadowed by the decision that was looming.

In 2007, that moment of truth finally arrived. A few days before the official lists of candidates for Congress were due to be presented, Humerto Tumini proposed that I represent the province of Buenos Aires on the ticket of the Frente para la Victoria, the electoral coalition founded by the Kirchners. The matter was decided in a matter of hours, and two days later I became the official no. 18 on the slate of candidates. This time I was elected outright, becoming the youngest representative in Argentine history. Even taking my two different birth certificates into account!

But the elections of 2007 were not the start of a life definitively exposed to the media; they were more the culmination, even the crowning moment, of a process that had begun with my personal decision to authorize the media to contact me.

I had given my first interview to Victoria Ginzberg, from the newspaper *Página/12,* and that was the beginning of my climb into the spotlight. Although I've grown more comfortable with it since, those first steps were very hard, and if there was a first moment of silence and tears, it didn't get any better the second time around. With television programs, public meetings side by side with the Grandmothers of the Plaza de Mayo, and interviews, I was sure that sooner or later the tide would pass and that I'd slowly return to my semi-anonymous life as an activist, but I was wrong. Completely.

In early 2007, timed to coincide with the anniversary of

the coup d'état of 1976, the program *Televisión por la Identidad* (Television for Identity), coproduced by the Grandmothers of the Plaza de Mayo, made its debut. There were three parts to the series, two features and one documentary. The first one was based on the story of Tatiana Ruarte Britos, a granddaughter found by the Grandmothers in 1980, while the dictatorship was still in force. The second told the story of Juan Cabandié, and the third followed several different stories, with interviews at the end featuring a number of different grandchildren who had been traced, including me.

Not long after, there was a theater piece called *Vic y Vic*, written by Erika Halvorsen, with two characters based on my friend Vicky Grigera and me, that recounts their stories, the lives of their missing parents, and their experiences. It was especially gratifying to take part in the creation of this work and to contribute information to it, because Vicky, now a professional actress, played herself. The play opened at the Complejo La Plaza, as part of a series called "For the Sake of Identity."

Jaime's documentary finally saw the light of day one year later, also on the anniversary of the coup, after overcoming all sorts of threats, break-ins, and denunciations. Even though I had been part of it from the beginning and had seen bits and pieces of it while it was in production, when I saw it projected publicly for the first time, I felt as if I had finally made the transition: too many things had happened since I found out the truth about my identity, and that film represented a new beginning in my life. Victoria, who had been gradually coming into her own throughout that time, could finally accept herself, define herself, internalize Analía, and move on.

To a certain extent, if the year 2004 precipitated an earthquake that shook the very foundations of my identity, the year 2007 closed that cycle with a force that was equally intense. When everything started to come apart, my political activity became a clear, well-defined sphere in which my beliefs were no longer affected by the changes in my life. By the same token, it was those very changes that gradually transformed me into a public persona, one more symbol of the blackest period in Argentine history. Those two utterly separate spheres, that of the political activist and that of the daughter of *desaparecidos*, converged in 2007.

My public exposure increased in proportion with my political activities: the documentary, the threats and public accusations against my uncle by the Grandmothers of the Plaza de Mayo, the series *Televisión por la Identidad*, the play, the interviews, and the television programs were all jockeying for room in a schedule that was already overbooked with the activities of the Claudia Falcone project, the Avellaneda City Council, and the National Department for Youth. And in the midst of that *mare magnum* in which I had lost all control, I was asked to stand as a candidate for representative to the national Congress, an honor I accepted after consulting with my *compañeros* in the party, and especially with my beloved friend Humberto Tumini. I can see us again, seated at a table in a café, asking whether my parents would have approved if I ran, knowing how much contempt they had for the electoral path.

He patiently assured me that this was a different time now and the forms of struggle were different too, so with the confidence I've always had in him and that I'll always have, I accepted the challenge, with the knowledge that I would never be alone to face it. It wasn't until after the October election, when I realized what lay ahead, that the crisis really hit me: after years of working with the patience of an ant to carve out my own political space, had I now become a congressperson just because I was the daughter of *desaparecidos*? Was that what I had become?

On top of the doubts I had about the job, there was the sacrifice it implied. Being a representative was a full-time job, which meant I would have to stop working at the Claudia Falcone project. Community organizing was what had led me to politics. The need to do something concrete and to support real human beings had been my compass ever since my days in the church youth group. Now, in order to continue in politics, that was exactly what I was going to have to give up. Although I've since overcome my lack of confidence about being a legislator, I'll never get over my frustration at no longer being able to work with people in the trenches. Over time, I've come to understand that it's all one project with the same set of ideas. I realize this is just a new chapter in my life, one in which I have the opportunity to build something politically and to contribute from another angle, neither more nor less important than before, just different. And I'm fortified by the conviction that if this stage comes to an end, I'll be happy to return to what I was doing all along, which directly or indirectly brought me to this moment.

As to why I was elected to Congress, I've learned to think differently about that too. After all, the answer to whether I was elected as a daughter of the disappeared is most certainly yes. That was not the only reason, and it doesn't define me, but it's certainly undeniable. Nor do I doubt that many people expected me to be a passive symbol in Congress, someone who would raise her hand when told to and nothing more. But I've learned that what matters is not the reasons behind my candidacy but the role I can play as a lawmaker and what I can contribute from the position to which I was elected. Being the daughter of *desaparecidos* and the first recovered grandchild to serve in the Chamber of Deputies is also a mandate that entails enormous responsibilities.

From the Commission on Human Rights, of which I'm the secretary, I've proposed and supported projects that help shed light on events that occurred during the last dictatorship, that call for justice and that guarantee the words that became the slogan of the human rights community once democracy had been restored: "Never Again." Projects such as the ineligibility for public office of those who took part in the state terrorism of the last dictatorship, or the implementation of a system of witness protection, are consistent with the mandate on which I was elected, both as the daughter of *desaparecidos* and as a representative of the Movimientos Libres del Sur—namely, to strengthen democratic institutions.

But my activity in Congress isn't limited to human rights, and takes my role well beyond that of a symbol of the disappeared. Two projects that represent advances for Argentine society are the expropriation of the Hotel Bauen, built during the dictatorship and declared bankrupt when a judge vacated his order, and the modification of the Education Law that was drafted under Menem's presidency and that led to the virtual collapse of our education system. Pursuing such projects and others like them is part of the responsibility I accepted when I became a representative. In addition to my duties as a member of the congressional committee on human rights, I also sit on the committees for education, women, prison legislation, addiction prevention, cooperative affairs, and internal security. In all these capacities I seek to bring my experience, my ideas, and my work to the table. If being the daughter of *desaparecidos* makes me any different from my colleagues, it's because I demand a higher level of commitment from myself.

After facing a newly revealed truth, or a lie that had been unmasked, I had to gradually learn to internalize a new history, a new family, and a new past. Throughout that process, I repeatedly found myself unable to move forward, rejecting what had seemed valid to me before, and even at times rejecting myself. That process, which I like to think culminated in the elections of 2007, is approaching a point where I feel able to reconcile myself with everything that brought me here—good and bad, truth and lies. I'm just as much a product of the dictatorship as I am of the affection I received from Raúl and Graciela, and I recognize myself as much in them as I do in Cori and El Cabo, whom I love as much as it's possible to love someone you never met. I'm no less the niece of the former head of intelligence at the ESMA, who was there when his brother and sister-in-law were murdered, than I am that teenage girl who went into ecstatic fits at concerts of the Caballeros de la Quema. All of which means, above all, that I'm no less Analía than I am Victoria.

It goes without saying that my story still has its gaps, which is true for my parents and so many of the other disappeared. There is still much to be resolved, but I'm at peace with myself, and I firmly believe that one day I'll be able to learn the whole truth. After all, even with the murder of Febrés, who had to have known what happened to the babies born on his watch in the Sardá at the ESMA, there are many others who participated in this story. Among them my uncle, who is probably the only one who knows exactly what happened to my parents.

As to my sister Daniela, I don't think the last word has been said, but this is not the moment for us to see each other face-to-face again. She and I have already glimpsed the truth; it's here between the two of us. But it can't be imposed on another human being if she's not willing to see it. For now, Daniela has chosen not to open her eyes.

When this edition of the book comes out it will have been thirty-five years since the coup d'état that changed the life of Argentines forever. I had to wait twenty-seven years to learn the truth. Others waited less. But all of us together still don't know the whole story. We do our best to reconstruct it out of fragments, suppositions, and small discoveries that become pieces in a giant jigsaw puzzle. The ones who can solve it are those who took part in the dictatorship and committed the crimes. For years they were untouchable under the law, beyond the reach of people who demanded to know the whereabouts of their children, siblings, spouses, or parents. But since 2003 there has been a new political will from within the state, and the last barriers that propped up the laws of impunity have finally given way. Trials have resumed, and many of those once believed untouchable are now behind bars awaiting sentencing, or already sentenced to long jail terms. This is a historic moment in Argentina, and it's vital that we press on and not allow it to dissipate, since what's at stake is for us to know our true history—because a country without history is a country without a future.

Much remains to be done: gigantic cases such as the megacase of the ESMA have languished for years in some drawer of the Justice Department, where there are still holdover appointees with little incentive to expose the atrocities of state terrorism they themselves rubber-stamped. The majority of military prisoners are enjoying house arrest or are being held in military jails, where they are treated like royalty by their brothers-in-arms. Cases such as the murder of Febrés or the kidnapping of Julio López—a former detainee and torture victim who disappeared in 2006, after testifying against Miguel Etchecolatz, a senior police officer during the dictatorship—show to what lengths the death squads of the 1970s are willing to go and the degree of impunity with which they are still able to act, protected by the mafias that profited so handsomely back in the day. Even within democratic institutions it's hard at times to move forward with everybody going in the same direction, as has been clear from our project to prevent former members of the last dictatorship from holding public posts. Of course, it's inevitable that there are always players with a stake in hiding the truth, but political determination and will have proven to be powerful weapons in the fight for justice.

And it is perhaps in this way—by portraying the role of determination through the narrative of my personal story— that this book can make the greatest contribution. Obviously, my story is not a typical one, but neither is it unique. Give or take a few bumps along the way, a little more or a little less violence and more or less information, and my story is the same as that of five hundred other children born in captivity or kidnapped along with their parents under the dictatorship. It's also the story of the thirty thousand Argentine men and women, most of them young, who were victims of the torture and terrorism of the state. And it is the story of thirty million Argentines whose lives, to a greater or lesser degree, were affected by the dictatorship—because they had to go into exile and leave their loved ones behind, because they survived torture and must now live with the guilt of not having died a hero's death, or because they chose to ignore what was going on and today must face the horrors they did not allow themselves to see.

My story, the story of Analía and Victoria, of Cori and El Cabo, has meaning only when surrounded by the other thirty million stories that are alive today in Argentina. I'm sure this book will show many people the atrocities this country was capable of committing, and the way in which the facts are still hidden. It may even stun those who believed this was all over and done with thirty years ago, especially in a country that has always claimed to be the cultural light of Latin America, the place where the dichotomy between "civilization and barbarity" was dissolved long ago. For others, my story may only awaken a sense of horror at "how terrible the world is," while still others may even find it impossible to relate to, because the narrator may strike them at times as too stubborn and willful. But my objective in writing this book has been fulfilled. I realize that what happened to me may be more or less acceptable, and it may arouse revulsion or sympathy. But in every case, what I've told here is the truth. This happened. It happened in a way that transcends my own story to embrace the thirty million other stories. It happened in Argentina, barely thirty years ago, and it happened to all of us. This book is just one more case. One more example, we might say. An example of the horror, and of the fatal consequences of dictatorship.

As for me, my job is to keep moving forward and learning. Today my political activity has renewed meaning within the story of my parents, and in their legacy, in all that I carried inside me but that took decades for me to understand. After all the times when I felt helpless even just to move, today I feel stronger than ever and prouder to be who I am, the daughter of Cori and El Cabo. I hope my story will be useful to someone, and that it can contribute on a larger scale to the realization that the truth can be hidden or changed, or people can even try to destroy it, but it will always rise to the surface, because the truth can't be held back forever. And I hope this will become but one among the hundreds of other stories that remain to be told, which belong to all the children who still have no idea of their identity and who are living a fiction and a lie that they will one day, sooner or later, overturn.

Today I feel that the desert is behind me, and that if I owe myself anything it's to live my life from now on savoring each moment, because I know I am complete. To live will always mean to continue the fight for the truth, and for what I consider just—for my convictions.

I owe this to my parents, who gave their lives to build a more just world for their daughters. I owe it to Analía, who had no choice but to succumb and sacrifice herself so that the truth could take its place in the story. I owe it to all those who supported me and stood by me to make sure I didn't fall apart. And I owe it to myself, as the product of a novelesque plot that began before I was born.

After all, despite the certainty that they would steal her daughter, despite imagining that her husband had been killed and that she herself would not live long after giving birth, Cori sent her killers a message by giving me a name and identifying me. In that symbolic act of defiance, Cori lives on, and that has become my legacy.

Her last cry is in my name, her last stubborn refusal of the fate that had been imposed on her. Because my existence proves that in the end Cori achieved her goal, and that Cori won her last round. That's why my name is Victoria.

# Afterword
## WE ARE ALL PERONISTS
### by Pablo A. Pozzi

There is a well-known story about Argentina's ex-president, General Juan Domingo Perón: once upon a time a foreign ambassador asked Perón to describe Argentine politics. Perón thought about it for a short while and, with a huge smile on his face, said: "Well, my friend, in Argentina 30 percent are *radicales*, another 30 percent are conservatives, 20 percent are Socialists, 10 percent Communists, and there are 10 percent who really do not care about politics." "But that is 100 percent," responded a surprised ambassador. "What about the Peronists?" "Oh no, we are all Peronists," said Perón, laughing.[1]

Though the story is probably not true, the fact is that it represents the main problem in explaining what Peronism really is, both for Argentines and foreigners. Peronism seems to be everything for everyone, and its story is complex while at the same time crucial to understanding political events in Argentina over the past sixty years.

Peronism joined together "old" and "new" workers with the more conservative middle classes in small towns and with businessmen geared to the domestic market. At the same time, it was supported by the Catholic Church and absorbed a portion of the traditional parties. For instance, the Socialist Federation of Tucumán, the Unión Cívica Radical Junta Renovadora, and a large sector of the Córdoba province conservatives joined Peronism. Perón's vice-presidential candidate, Hortensio Quijano, was a prominent UCR politician.

In reality the problem in explaining Peronism was due to the fact that it was a new social and political phenomenon and, as such, had a syncretic quality such that it took bits from every previous Argentine political tradition. The result was that many people felt *peronista*, always relating to some aspect of its conflicting and contradictory ideas. When asked what Peronism was, they would respond "*es un sentimiento*" (it is a sentiment or feeling). Thus, in Perón's first government, the first foreign minister (Atilio Bramuglia) was a Socialist lawyer while his successor (Gerónimo Remorino) was a prominent conservative; the minister of interior (Angel Borlenghi) was a Socialist labor leader; the minister for war (José Humberto Sosa Molina) was a right-wing military officer; the minister of education (Oscar Ivanissevich) was a nationalist Catholic admirer of Franco's Spain. This plasticity and ability to absorb contradictory and different ideas has permitted Peronism to survive and to retain a proteanlike centrality in Argentine politics.

Juan Domingo Perón was an obscure army colonel of conservative political inclinations. In 1943, as part of a secret organization[2] of nationalist army officers, Perón took part in the coup d'état that overthrew the government of President Ramón Castillo. At the time, however, Perón was not among the main leaders of the coup. The new military dictatorship was headed by Generals Pedro Pablo Ramírez and Edelmiro Farrell, and Perón was appointed secretary of labor, a relatively unimportant and powerless post. Between 1943 and 1945 he was able to rise within the military regime to vice president. In the process he forged an alliance with labor and small and middle businessmen that would allow him to win the presidential elections in February 1946, and overshadow Argentine politics for the next sixty years, even after his death in 1974.

The rise of Perón and the emergence of Peronism can be traced to the changes in Argentina caused by the world crisis of 1929. In 1930, as a young lieutenant, Perón was one of the officers who overthrew the popular government of UCR President Hipólito Yrigoyen. Between 1931 and 1943 Argentine elections were defined by what many journalists termed *el fraude patriótico* (patriotic fraud), while corruption and violence became rife in the landowner-controlled government. It was also a period of hard-fought strikes, and savage repression. The Argentine police inaugurated the use of the electric cattle prod to torture labor activists in 1930. This period became known in Argentine history as the *Década Infame* (Infamous Decade).

At the same time, the 1929 crisis had a huge impact on Argentine society and its economy, since it curtailed beef and wheat exports to industrialized nations such as Great Britain. This generated changes with far-reaching effects. On the one hand, industrial imports had to be substituted with lower-quality local products due to the fact that there were less foreign currencies available to acquire imports. The reduction in agricultural exports, while local industries grew, led to rural unemployment and migration toward the cities in search of jobs. One of the results of this migration was the growth of trade unions and of the Communist Party. Communists organized and led large industrial unions, such as those for meatpackers and construction workers; both of these unions organized mostly the "new" migrant workers. The emergence of "Red" unions, the rise in the number of hard-fought strikes, and the danger of social upheaval marked Colonel Perón's worldview. To him, and many other army officers, Fascism seemed the best option to stem the "Red challenge."

When World War II started, in 1939, the political elite and the officer corps split between those who were pro Axis and those, such as the navy, who were pro British and French. Unable to resolve the situation, they settled on neutrality as logical foreign policy. Once the Germans were defeated at the Battle of Stalingrad, in 1943, it became evident that they would lose the war. In Argentina, the pro-Allies faction seemed to become dominant. As a result the GOU overthrew the government in order to maintain neutrality.[3] The leaders of the new dictatorship soon faced the problem that the war was ending, that Argentina would see its exports reduced, and that the United States (whose economy was competitive and not complementary to Argentina's) would emerge as the main world power. In addition, faced with the prospect of a new round of Socialist revolutions similar to when World War I ended in 1918, they were concerned that the Communist Party and the Left in general had become predominant among the workers.

In the meantime the United States government accused the new military dictatorship of being Fascist, and threw all its support against it. In cooperation with this policy, the State Department and the U.S. Embassy in Buenos Aires became overtly involved in Argentine politics. By 1945 it was obvious that Perón had emerged as the main leader of the new regime, and would be its presidential candidate in the 1946 elections. In opposition, the UCR, Conservatives, Socialists, and Communists formed a coalition support-ing the candidacy of a *radical* politician. The State Depart-ment produced a white paper that termed Perón a Fascist, and gave monetary support to the opposing coalition. The white paper was written by then-ambassador to Argentina Spruille Braden, who later served as assistant secretary of state for Western Hemisphere affairs under Harry Truman. The report was leaked to the Argentine press together with a photostat of a check that the U.S. government sent to the anti-Peronist candidate. The result was a nationalist reaction in popular opinion, and the election was put in terms of "Braden or Perón." Perón won with more than fifty percent of the vote.

Previously, in 1944, Perón and the nationalist officers had decided to reorganize Argentina's economy and society. At the time, in the Americas, newspapers and parties debated the foundations of a much-desired democratic revival and depicted the government of Franklin D. Roosevelt as a model to be followed. In spite of being influenced by Mus-solini, who had just lost the war, Perón was concerned with avoiding the dangers of revolution and civil war. Thus, he came to admire the New Deal reforms of the U.S. president as a way to check the Left while attaining economic growth. Perón's basic idea was to increase employment, raise incomes, guarantee small and middle business profits and development, and facilitate credit. This would be fueled by redirecting earnings from the agricultural sector toward industry, especially small and middle businesses. At the same time, in order to protect national industry and jobs, he restricted foreign imports. Using the New Deal as a guideline, especially the Wagner Act, Perón legalized unionization and instituted a series of laws that protected labor bargaining and organizing. By 1946 most Argentines supported the implementation of policies similar to those of Roosevelt. In light of this, Perón was fairly successful in presenting himself as the Argentine version of the U.S. president.[4] Not surprisingly, however, these policies generated conflict with the traditional elites, especially the landowners and those businessmen geared toward exports. Labor and small and middle businessmen, in contrast, were supportive.

The combination of support from labor, social reforms, and progressive discourse generated a mystique that tended to obscure the less savory aspects of the new political movement and its leader. Perón, personally, was a very conservative and authoritarian person, always uncomfortable with the progressive elements of Peronism. His government repressed dissent, especially that from the Left. However, he was always a pragmatist. He would say: "I have a right hand because I have a left one." His policies tended to be pendular, always supporting one faction against the other so as to maintain his leadership within the movement. At the same time, he would make cryptic pronouncements that tended to define Argentine politics always in contradictory and undefined terms. For instance, one of the Twenty Peronist Truths was: "There is nothing better for a Peronist than another Peronist." This clearly excluded those who did not share allegiance to the leader, while another insisted that "Peronism desires national unity not struggle." Yet another stated that "Peronism wants a socially just, an economically free, and a politically sovereign nation."[5] The main Peronist slogan at the time was: "Neither Yankees nor Marxists, Peronists." A Peronist labor leader expressed to this writer, a few years later: "Well, we are really against all sorts of Reds; the part about Yanks is just a slogan."

Whatever Peron's political inclinations, under Peronism the lot of the average working person improved significantly. For instance, workers gained job stability through the requirement that employers pay a substantial indemnity to those fired without cause, and they also obtained paid vacations and maternity leave. Thus, though many "old Peronistas" recognized Perón's contradictions by saying that "he is a sly fox," they also believed that the movement could constrain the leader's conservative proclivities. These improvements and reforms led its supporters to believe that Peronism was a "national movement," embodying a revolution premised on a truly Argentine ideology in opposition to "foreign ideological imports" such as Liberalism and Communism.

However, Perón's main problem at the time was that Argentine labor had a strong leftist tradition. As he wrote in 1950:

> I spoke to them a bit in communism [*sic*]. Why? Because if I had spoken in any other language they would have pelted me with oranges [ . . . ] Because they were men with forty years of Marxism and with Communist leaders [ . . . ] They wanted to go where they thought was convenient [ . . . ] They believed in class struggle [ . . . ] The people who followed me did not want to go where I was going; they wanted to go their own way. I did not tell them where to go; I started walking ahead of them in the direction they wanted to go. Eventually, as we traveled together, I started to turn and took them where I wanted to go.[6]

Soon many labor activists realized that Perón was not heading where they wanted to go, and others wanted to follow beyond the limits he imposed. Starting in 1948 there were a series of hard-fought strikes that were repressed by the national government. An old Peronist activist of the Tucumán Sugar Workers Union (FOTIA) remembered the 1949 strike: "There I was, listening to Perón on the radio. He said our strike was a Communist conspiracy and started naming the Reds who had infiltrated our union. He mentioned my son's godfather. I said, 'He cannot enter my house ever again. I will not have Reds here.' Then he mentioned my name. I started crying. I did not understand. We were Peronists."[7]

Feeling threatened both by those outside his movement, who demanded a return to traditional politics, and those inside who wanted to "deepen the revolution," Perón unleashed repression on leftist activists, threatened traditional politicians, tightened government control of unions, and exercised media control. In addition, public employment became contingent on Peronist Party affiliation. Opposition and dissent were curtailed and not tolerated. Still today, in the Buenos Aires suburb of Lanús, neighbors remember don Lolo, an elderly Italian worker who, on the day Eva Perón died (in 1952), put a black band on his crotch. He promptly received a ten-day jail sentence for "disrespecting national symbols."

Perón had won the 1946 elections by a huge majority that only got bigger when he was reelected in 1952. In 1947 Peronism granted women the vote, and in 1949 a new Constitution enshrined many of the social safeguards. Taking a page from Roosevelt's last speech, Peronism declared that the right to work was constitutional, and that "private property was inviolate as long as it did not harm the greater social good." As a result labor increased its demands while the elite and the Catholic Church, with the support of the United States Embassy in Buenos Aires[8], began to plot a coup d'état. In June 1955, navy flyers bombed the Presidential Palace, killing hundreds of bystanders. And in September, the Third Army Corps rebelled in the city of Córdoba. The fate of the coup hung in the balance for seven days, while army rebels and loyalists fought. The labor confederation, the CGT, demanded weapons to defend the government and was refused. In the end, a rebellious navy sailed into Buenos Aires harbor and threatened to shell the city. Perón, concerned that the situation would turn into a full-scale civil war (akin to the Spanish Civil War), boarded a Paraguayan gunboat and went into exile for eighteen years.

The new regime quickly annulled the 1949 Constitution and tried unsuccessfully to rescind many of the reforms. The 1955 coup seared itself into the Argentine psyche. Mario, a former auto worker in Córdoba, recounted: "I will never forget the 1955 Revolution. An armored car parked in front of my home. I was playing in the street, and it crushed my spinning top. It was a sign. That was when the bad times began. The streets turned gray. You could feel people's sadness."[9]

Peronism left behind a changed Argentina. Since the 1930s Argentina has been an unusual Third World nation. Economically it had developed a strong industrial base geared mostly toward consumer products for a protected domestic market. Argentine industry fueled its growth with the foreign currency obtained through agricultural and beef exports produced by a few large landowning families, often at odds with protectionist policies but without sufficient political strength to overturn them. By the 1960s these families had become linked to foreign industrial and banking interests in Argentina and were able to destabilize elected governments in order to push forth their own economic agenda. At the same time, the growth of the State sector of the economy, the creation of a welfare state under the first Peronist government (1946–1955), and the fact that the State generated much of the domestic demand for goods and services, turned it into a key economic player and an area of hard-fought battles over its control. In addition, for many Argentines irrespective of their political sympathies, the ideal society was that of 1948 to 1949: high wages, low unemployment, job protection, free quality education, paid vacations, paid maternity leave, easy mortgages and credit, and a high level of consumption. Between 1955 and 1976, Argentine society split around these issues: the elite wanted to do away with them, while the majority of the population wanted to keep them. For many in the working and lower middle classes, Perón was the guarantee that the system worked out in 1948 would continue intact. This meant that political candidates who rejected this arrangement were unable to win free elections. One response by the elite was to make Peronism illegal and prohibit from electoral participation any political party affiliated with it. Another response was the overthrow of all governments elected during that period, in order to try to apply free-market economic and social policies. This was a period of dictatorial regimes that constrained political freedoms.

Peronism survived, not so much as an organized political movement or a coherent ideology, but as an allegiance to Perón and a bygone era, especially among workers. Thus, Fascists, moderates, and Marxists all could coexist within this broad and mostly unorganized movement. Each political tendency formed small organizations, all claiming to be Peronist. Since trade unions organized most workers, and many workers felt themselves to be Peronists, Labor adopted the joint tasks of representing workers at the bargaining table and

Peronists within the political sphere. Trade unions became, as Perón said, "Peronism's backbone" whose leaders would represent Perón and relay his instructions. Simultaneously, in spite (or perhaps because) of the leader's absence, Peronism developed a peculiar mythical quality as it became an expression not only for a "better world" but also an idea of popular worker dignity. This tradition, in reality nonexistent during the first Peronist government, was transmitted from parents to children. For instance, Mario again remembered:

> My father read us Peron's five-year plan. This became a goal for us. He said: this is the way we should live. Believer or not, I became a Peronist. So, after 1955 I was a Peronist soldier. At home we listened to Perón's speeches in the old records that *compañeros* brought home and that we played on our old victrola.
>
> In my fourth year of high school a professor taught us math. He claimed that to understand math you had to understand Peronism, and vice versa. So, class was an hour of Peronist politics and an hour of math. This professor only spoke of Perón's greatness and that the noblest thing was to work in an airplane factory . . . to make Argentina great. The professor also said that Peronists are only those who come from below.[10]

Economic changes had also brought about social, cultural, and political changes. By 1960, Argentina had developed a large middle class, which saw the State both as a channel for social mobility and as a source of jobs. The rural population was relatively small, most being either farmers (sharecroppers or small landholders) or wage earners (ranch hands and *peones*). Concurrently, steady industrial growth since the 1930s had created a large working class, organized into strong unions. Culturally many of these workers leaned to the Left, expressing their anti-imperialist and laborite feelings through Peronism. Both middle-class desires and working-class interests clashed with those of the foreign-oriented businessmen.

Thus, politically a majority of the working class and rural wage earners were Peronists, and the middle class tended toward the UCR, while the conservative bourgeoisie alternated between the two majority parties and small provincial political organizations. The Left included a sizeable Communist Party and smaller Trotskyist groups; both had little or no influence within the working class. As a whole this implied that while economic might was highly concentrated in few hands, the electoral system permitted the majority of the population to express its support for the socio-economic system worked out between 1945 and 1955. The result was a political stalemate, leading to instability over almost three decades, where no elected government was allowed to finish its term in office and where military dictatorships represented the interests of the highly concentrated economic power groups.

The result was a generalized feeling of injustice where the average citizen had no institutional possibilities for redress. Already in 1956, spontaneously, many Peronists had taken up civil disobedience. Others took up arms to demand Perón's return: commandos and guerrillas were common in the late

1950s. Government repression, and Perón's rejection of these methods, led to their failure by 1962. A new coup in 1962, and another in 1966, made sure that the feelings of political disenfranchisement remained. At the same time, the Cuban Revolution, Che Guevara, the Vietnam War, and the many guerrilla movements throughout Latin America added to the growing sense that armed struggle was part of a larger path toward social justice. Labor grew in militancy and many young Argentines became politicized toward the radicalized Left or the more militant Peronist options. In May 1969, in the city of Córdoba in central Argentina, a labor demonstration turned into street fighting where workers took control of the city for three days. The army was forced to battle street by street in order to regain control. To this day we do not know how many people died in Córdoba, but its impact on the nation was immeasurable. In the following three years there were similar uprisings in many Argentine cities.

One of the key aspects revealed by the uprising, known as the *Cordobazo*, was that Peronism's hold on workers had weakened considerably. Perón had already tried to return in 1965. He was stopped in Brazil and prevented from reaching Argentina. Though he still retained very significant support, the incident revealed that Peronist militancy had cooled: there was no mass mobilization to support his return. Rank-and-file workers were now challenging traditional Peronist labor leaders, while many young union activists were turning to different strands of Marxism.

In addition, the Cordobazo had turned the small armed groups that had existed underground into a ready supply of active guerrillas. Between 1969 and 1972 more than twenty guerrilla groups operated in Argentina, among them several who considered themselves both Peronist and Marxist, and posited Perón's return as the first step toward a Socialist revolution. Perón, ever the pragmatist, leaned to the Left; he sent regards to Fidel Castro, spoke highly of Mao Tse-tung and Ho Chi Minh, and said: "If I were young I would also be in the streets throwing bombs."

Though Argentines from all social classes and of all ages became militant, it was mostly those from fifteen to thirty who responded. Many became guerrillas; others joined the many Marxist groups. The Juventud Peronista Regionales (Regional Peronist Youth), led by the Montonero Peronist guerrillas, became one of the largest organizations at the time. It was here that the mysticism of "Perón, the revolutionary," fostered over the past decade and a half, attracted thousands of young Argentines. As said Ernesto, a former Montonero: "I remember seeing Perón . . . it was like a drug to listen to Perón, and you said you have to do something . . . we felt like glory. It was a really strong thing, mystical, of historical force. If you ask me if I ever liked guns, I have to say I did not. I did not like violence; I never was interested in arms. But at the time it was like a natural thing that historical commitment would push you in that direction. It was immoral to stand aside. It was saying, 'Well, we are doing something historically important where social justice is a real possibility and only a son of bitch can remain outside the struggle. How could you reject this popular project and the like?' It was a very strong emotional thing."

Perón's tactic was successful. By 1972, the dictatorship begun in 1966 was forced to call elections, removed the ban on Peronist participation, and permitted Perón's return in the hope that the old leader could control what seemed like a slide toward socialism. After all, he had always said that "you get on the horse from the left, and off from the right," meaning that in Argentina you win elections by posing as a leftist and you govern as a conservative. The Peronist Youth (Juventud Peronista), a surface organization of the Montonero Peronist guerrillas, played a central role in the electoral campaign, helping secure the election of Peronist congresspersons and provincial governors. In May 1973 Héctor Cámpora, an old-fashioned Peronist politician who had won the elections with 49 percent of the vote and became president of Argentina, resigned after fifty days to allow Perón himself to stand for office. In September 1973 the old leader was elected president while his third wife, "Isabelita" (María Estela Martínez), became vice president.

Perón remained an essentially conservative politician who was concerned about the leftward drift in his movement, in spite of the fact that most guerrillas had declared a truce and supported his government. Just like in 1948, his solution was to stifle dissent and unofficially repress the very same people who believed his return was the antechamber to revolution. Perón and his wife obtained the appointment of José López Rega as the new minister of social welfare. This former policeman organized the Argentine Anticommunist Alliance or Triple A, a paramilitary group whose task was to root out the insurgency. López Rega relied on the right-wing nationalist tendencies of

Peronism. Groups such as Guardia de Hierro (Iron Guard), Comando de Organización (Organization Commando), the Juventud Sindical Peronista (Peronist Trade Union Youth), and the Juventud Peronista de la República Argentina (Peronist Youth of the Argentine Republic) took up the call to defend the leader from "the Reds who had infiltrated the movement." Supported by the police, the Army Intelligence Service, and by most Peronist labor leaders, they unleashed a campaign of terror on progressive and left-wing politicians and activists, as well as on Marxist and Peronist guerrillas.

Most progressive Peronists rationalized the violence they were suffering at the hands of the government they had elected by positing "the theory of encirclement." This meant that Perón sympathized with progressive goals, but was unable to see what was happening due to the advisors who surrounded him. Thus, these progressives saw it as their task to "rescue" their leader. They were soon disabused of this notion. Perón died on July 1, 1974, but not before confronting the left wing of his movement in a speech he gave on May 1. The plaza in front of the Presidential Palace was filled with thousands of Peronist Youth who suddenly started chanting: "What has happened, what has happened, General? The popular government is full of *gorilas*."[11] Perón responded by berating "beardless" youth who were disrespectful of labor leaders. Thousands turned their backs on him and left the plaza.

His death unleashed a confrontation between Peronist guerrillas, allied to armed Marxist organizations, and the right wing of the Peronist movement led by now President Isabel Perón and López Rega. A year after Peron's death, the two largest armed organizations, the People's Revolutionary Army (Guevarist) and the Montoneros (Peronists) had a cadre of some six thousand, plus thousands more organized in their periphery. These organizations led unions and set up women's groups and neighborhood associations, as well as newspapers, publishing houses, and even arms factories. Labor was also affected: the established leaders who had reached an accommodation with the dictatorships were now challenged by rank-and-file insurgencies.

To prevent the continued growth of these organizations, by mid-1975 the Triple A had murdered congresspersons, leftist labor leaders, a prominent lawyer and philosopher and brother of a former Argentine president, progressive priests, and hundreds of activists. In addition, the Peronist government called on the armed forces to participate in repressing the Left including guerrillas, progressive Catholic priests, and labor activists. As chaos ensued, popular mobilization was halted, while guerrilla activity increased and the armed forces waited on the sidelines. Many right-wing Peronist and UCR politicians, and the leadership of the trade unions, began plotting with the military to overthrow Isabelita Perón and bring "order" to the nation.[12]

The 1976 coup unleashed a level of repression previously unseen in Argentine history. At the same time, the elites took advantage and rolled back most social protections and welfare benefits. Human rights organizations estimate that the dictatorship caused 30,000 disappearances, about 8,000 deaths, jailed some 10,000 persons, and forced tens of thousands into exile. Working-class resistance went underground

and succeeded in blocking many military policies.[13] A further result of this resistance was that one of the goals of
the dictatorship—to generate a new political consensus—
became impossible. However, because of the sheer massive-
ness of the repression, the resistance remained atomized and
unable to unify into a political alternative to the dictatorship.
When Argentina, in 1983, returned to elections and the military were forced to withdraw after the fiasco of the Malvinas/
Falkland Islands War, the Left emerged defeated and with serious problems, but with a mass following expressed by its
collective 10 percent of the electoral vote, making it a significant player in electoral politics. In addition, the military left
the nation in a state of economic disarray with a speculative
economy, deindustrialization, and a huge foreign debt.[14]

Argentina returned to a democratic form of government
after a long and harsh seven-year dictatorship. For most
Argentines 1983 was a year of hope and confidence in the
future. Political participation was high as was social activism. Raúl Alfonsín, a leader of the center-right Radical Civic
Union (UCR) was elected president on a progressive platform.[15] Believing that popular disaffection with the dictatorship could generate a new round of revolutionary upheavals,
during the electoral campaign Alfonsín took up many of the
demands made by the Left under the dictatorship.[16] One
of his major achievements was to bring to trial, and condemn, the members of the military junta that had headed
the dictatorship. However, once he became president he had
little chance to carry out even his limited reformist program,
for he was subjected to both economic destabilization and

military pressures. Between 1983 and 1989 there were three military uprisings,[17] which succeeded in obtaining concessions from the government. In addition, big business refused to support any economic policy intended to limit speculation as the main form of capital accumulation. After 1985 Alfonsín caved in to economic pressures and adopted a neoconservative outlook in his economic policies, including wage freezes and the privatization of the State sector. However, labor opposed this, and carried out thirteen general strikes. This represented both rank-and-file pressure and the fact that most trade union leaders were Peronists, and thus members of the opposition party.

In 1989 Alfonsín was forced to hand over his office six months early, in the midst of hyperinflation, riots, and economic bankruptcy. His successor was Carlos Menem, a Peronist leader and governor of La Rioja province. Like Perón, Menem promised wage increases and a "production revolution" in order to get elected. Once in office, he "governed from the Right" and applied a whole series of neoconservative economic and social policies that were very similar to those implemented by the dictatorship. In addition, improvements in human rights were eschewed in favor of a pragmatic approach to power politics. Thus, between 1989 and 1990, with Alfonsín's support, Menem passed a series of laws putting an end to the trials for human rights violations. Eventually the dictators condemned in 1985 were freed and allowed to rejoin society. It would be twenty more years before these trials would resume, due to popular demand.

In the process, Peronism was also transformed from a heterogeneous movement into a formal political party controlled by a pragmatic right wing. Still, Perón's shadow and the myth of his "revolutionary" reforms of 1946 remain a desirable benchmark for many Argentines.

## NOTES

1. In Argentina *radicales* are members of the Unión Cívica Radical (UCR) party, a center-right, middle-class organization founded in 1890.
2. This was the GOU, and though it is not known exactly what the acronym stood for, it is believed to mean United Officers Group.
3. In spite of this, Argentina joined the war on the side of Allies in late 1944.
4. See Laura Ruiz Jiménez. "Peronism and Anti-imperialism in the Argentine Press: 'Braden or Perón' Was Also 'Perón Is Roosevelt.'" *Journal of Latin American Studies* (1998), 30: 551–571. Copyright © 1998 Cambridge University Press.
5. The *Veinte Verdades Peronistas* were read by Perón in a speech on October 17, 1950.
6. Juan Perón. *Conducción Política* (Buenos Aires: Mundo Peronista, 1950), 290.
7. Pablo A. Pozzi, interview with Graciela del Valle Romano, who remembered her uncle, Benito Romano, leader of FOTIA, Tucumán, Argentina, 1990.
8. For the conflictive relationship between the United States and the Perón government, see Harold F. Peterson. *La Argentina y los Estados Unidos* (Buenos Aires: EUDEBA, 1970).

9. Pablo A. Pozzi, interview with Mario, Córdoba, Argentina, February 28, 1994.

10. Pablo A. Pozzi, interview with Mario, Córdoba, Argentina, February 28, 1994. Perón would send speeches recorded on audio tapes and old 78 rpm "paste" records that were reverently listened to in working-class homes throughout the 1960s.

11. The word *gorila* was a popular term for anti-Peronists who supported military dictatorships. The May 1 protestors also chanted: "We were stupid, we were stupid, we voted for a whore, a wizard, and a cuckold." The reference was to popular belief that López Rega (also known as *El Brujo*, "the Wizard") was Isabel Perón's lover. Perón became incensed when he heard this chant.

12. There are a lot of studies on the 1976 coup. One of the more traditional, whose articles summarize different points of view and show levels of collusion between the military and political and labor elites, is Peter Waldmann y Ernesto Garzón Valéz (eds). *El poder militar en la Argentina 1976–1981.* (Buenos Aires: Editorial Galerna, 1982).

13. See Pablo A. Pozzi. *Oposición obrera a la dictadura.* (Buenos Aires: Editorial Contrapunto, 1988).

14. Argentina's foreign debt increased from five billion dollars in 1975 to 36 billion in 1983.

15. Campaign promises included respect for human rights, the rule of law, popular education, national industry protection, justice for those affected by the repression, diplomatic nonalignment and improvement of relations with the Third World, and economic development. The only campaign promise fulfilled was to try the members of the dictatorship's military junta for human rights abuses.

16. In spite of Alfonsín's progressive and democratic image, he has always been closer to the political right than to the center. For instance, throughout the 1976–1983 military dictatorship, he advised Minister for the Interior General Albano Harguindeguy (who was also his business partner) about many legal and political problems, especially in terms of how to deal with "the human rights issue."

17. There was a fourth one, in December 1989, under the Menem Administration.

# Chronology

*This chronology is not exhaustive. It is intended primarily to clar-ify the major events in the book.*

**JUNE 4, 1943:** Military coup d'état against the government of Ramón Castillo, organized by the GOU (Group of Officers United), one of whose leaders is Juan Domingo Perón. Known as the Revolution of '43, it heralded the rise of Perón and the start of Peronism.

**FEBRUARY 24, 1946:** Perón is elected president of Argentina.

**NOVEMBER 11, 1951:** Perón is elected to a second term.

**SEPTEMBER 16, 1955:** Coup d'état known as the "Liberating Revolution." Peronism is banned.

**JULY 1, 1970:** First public appearance of the Montoneros, who kidnap General Pedro Aramburu, one of the leaders of the Liberating Revolution, and then execute him after holding a revolutionary trial.

**JULY 30, 1970:** First public appearance of the FAR (Revolutionary Armed Forces), who seize the city of Garín in the province of Buenos Aires.

**OCTOBER 1973:** The Montoneros and the FAR join forces and take the name Montoneros.

**MARCH II, 1973:** Triumph of Peronism in the presidential elections, although without Perón, who remains in exile in Spain. Héctor Cámpora is elected president.

**JUNE 20, 1973:** Perón returns to Argentina. The Massacre of Ezeiza (Buenos Aires airport), armed clashes between the Montoneros and unionists allied with the Peronist right wing.

**OCTOBER 12, 1973:** Juan Domingo Perón is elected president in a third term following the resignation of Héctor Cámpora.

**NOVEMBER 21, 1973:** First attack by the Triple A in retaliation for a kidnapping organized by the Montoneros.

**MAY I, 1974:** Perón expels the Montoneros from the May I celebration in the Plaza de Mayo.

**JULY I, 1974:** Death of General Perón. His wife, María Estela Martínez de Perón (known as Isabel), becomes president with the support of the right wing of Peronism.

**SEPTEMBER 1974:** The Montoneros officially go underground.

**MARCH 24, 1976:** Coup d'état and the beginning of the last Argentine dictatorship, the bloodiest of all.

**MARCH 28, 1977:** Abduction of María Hilda Pérez de Donda. A few months later, her husband, José María Donda, is also seized.

**APRIL 2, 1982:** Beginning of the Falklands War, the dictatorship's last attempt at legitimization. The war ends two months later, with disastrous losses for Argentina.

**OCTOBER 30, 1983:** After almost eight years of dictatorship, during which thirty thousand people disappear, Raúl Alfonsín is elected president with 51.7 percent of the vote.

**SEPTEMBER 20, 1984:** Publication of the CONADEP (National Commission on the Disappearance of Persons) report containing the testimony of survivors and the accusations against members of the military that will provide the basis for their eventual trials.

**1985:** Trials of the military juntas. The leaders responsible for kidnapping and acts of torture committed under the dictatorship are found guilty. Legal proceedings against lower-ranking officers continue.

**DECEMBER 24, 1986:** Congress approves the Law of Final Stop, which puts a halt to the trials of former military men.

**JUNE 4, 1987:** Carlos Menem is elected president.

**OCTOBER 7, 1989:** Menem pardons jailed former military brass and Montonero leaders.

**DECEMBER 29, 1990:** Second series of presidential pardons. Those responsible for the genocide committed under the dictatorship as well as Montonero leaders are set free.

**MAY 14, 1995:** Reelection of Carlos Menem to the presidency, made possible by amending the Constitution one year earlier with the "Olive Pact," an agreement between the country's two main political parties, the Peronists and the Unión Cívica Radical (UCR).

**OCTOBER 24, 1999:** Fernando de la Rúa is elected president.

**DECEMBER 19 AND 20, 2001:** Exhausted by the economic crisis, Argentines turn out into the streets to protest, but slowly lose control over the situation. The riots are capped by looting and many deaths after being brutally put down by the police. Fernando de la Rúa resigns as president. A period of political uncertainty begins, with four different presidents leading the country in the space of a month.

**MARCH 27, 2003:** Néstor Kirchner is elected president after Carlos Menem, the other candidate, withdraws from a runoff contest between the two.

**AUGUST 2003:** Congress annuls the decrees of amnesty for former members of the military and declares the laws of Final Stop and Due Obedience unconstitutional. It now becomes possible to reopen the trials of those responsible for the atrocities committed during the last dictatorship, which as crimes against humanity have no statute of limitation.

**OCTOBER 28, 2007:** Cristina Fernández de Kirchner, wife of Néstor Kirchner, is elected president of Argentina. In the same vote, Victoria Donda is elected national representative for the province of Buenos Aires.

# Glossary

**Alfonsín, Raúl**   The first democratically elected president (1983–1989) after the fall of the military dictatorship. He assumed power with immense public support (the other candidate, Ítalo Lúder, a Peronist, had little chance of winning) and promised during his campaign to revoke the amnesty decree put in place by the junta's last president, Reynaldo Bignone. While the early years of his presidency ushered in the first trials of former members of the military, they were followed by the laws of Due Obedience and Final Stop, which absolved those guilty of crimes committed under the dictatorship and allowed the release of hundreds of torturers and killers. He resigned from the presidency five months before his term was up, due to popular pressure and inflation that had risen to over 3,000 percent.

**The Alliance (Alianza)**   A center-left coalition established ahead of the presidential elections of October 1999 by the Frente Grande (Broad Front), which brought together the Unión Cívica Radical (UCR) and independents and Peronists opposed to the neoliberal policies of Carlos Menem. In October, the Alliance candidates, Antonio de la Rúa and Carlos "Chacho" Alvarez, defeated the Peronist candidate, Eduardo Duhalde. Despite the expectations the new government created, the Alliance continued to apply the same policies as

231

Carlos Menem. In 2001, the economic crisis and popular riots led Fernando de la Rúa to exit the government, and a constitutional crisis ensued.

**Triple A (Argentine Anticommunist Alliance)** A paramilitary organization that functioned within the Peronist government of Isabel Perón. Created in 1973 by one of the most sinister faces of Peronism, José López Rega, during the interim presidency of Raúl Lastiri, its declared goal was to fight the forces of the revolutionary left at the time of their heyday in Argentina. It was able to count on the full support of the police and the power of the government. The Triple A was dismantled under the dictatorship and replaced by army death squads.

**Carlotto, Estela de** President of the Grandmothers of the Plaza de Mayo. She was a housewife with no interest in politics when her pregnant daughter was kidnapped in November 1977. In order to find her daughter and grandchild, she turned to the Grandmothers, and continues to search tirelessly for her grandson, Guido.

**Cavallo, Domingo** Secretary of the treasury under President Carlos Menem. He was the father of "convertibility," which allowed the Argentine peso and the U.S. dollar to remain at parity for ten years. Called back to his post by the government of Fernando de la Rúa, his disastrous management of the economy was affirmed by the antigovernment demonstrations known as the *cacerolazo* (the smashing of pots and pans) in December 2001, which ultimately led to his resignation.

**CDD (Centros Clandestinos de Detención, or Clandestine Detention Centers)**   Located for the most part in buildings that belonged to the army or police, these centers functioned as true concentration camps under the last dictatorship. There were approximately five hundred of them throughout Argentina. The most important ones were La Perla (in Córdoba), Campo de Mayo (in the province of Buenos Aires), and the Olimpo and the ESMA (the Naval Mechanics School), both in Buenos Aires.

**de la Rúa, Fernando**   Alliance candidate for the presidency, elected in 1999. From the start of his term, despite his campaign promises, he applied a neoliberal economic policy, appointing as his secretary of the treasury Domingo Cavallo, who had held the same post under Carlos Menem. Two years into his presidency, with the economic crisis growing steadily worse, he catalyzed middle-class ire by freezing savings accounts. He resigned following the *cacerolazo* (demonstrations), which were brutally repressed by the police on December 19 and 20, 2001.

**ERP (Ejército Revolucionario del Pueblo—People's Revolutionary Army)**   A guerrilla movement founded in Argentina in 1970, more nationalist and more inclined to follow the teachings of Che Guevara than the Montoneros were. Mario Roberto Santucho, their leader, was killed in 1976 in a roundup organized by the military. By the time of the junta, the ERP was already weakened and on its way to disappearing.

**ESMA (Escuela Superior de Mecánica de la Armada—Superior School of Naval Mechanics)**   A property located in the northern section of the city of Buenos Aires, on Libertador Avenue, deeded to the army in 1924 for the purpose of educating officers and sub-officers of the navy. During the last dictatorship, the Officers' Mess at the ESMA housed one of the largest underground detention centers. Of the more than five thousand prisoners held at the ESMA, only a hundred survived. On March 24, 2004, the buildings were returned to the city of Buenos Aires in order to house the Museum of Memory and a number of other cultural centers administered by various human rights organizations.

**Grandmothers of the Plaza de Mayo (Abuelas de la Plaza de Mayo)** Once part of the Mothers of the Plaza de Mayo, this association was created in 1977 when twelve women whose grandchildren were among the disappeared—either born in prison or abducted along with their parents—filed petitions of habeas corpus on suspicion that the children had been illegally adopted. Along with other human rights organizations, the Grandmothers have worked tirelessly to find more than one hundred of the five hundred originally missing.

**HIJOS (Hijos por la Identidad y la Justicia, Contra el Olvido y el Silenco, or Sons and Daughters for Identity and Against Oblivion and Silence)** Association established in 1995 by sons and daughters of the disappeared. Together with the Grandmothers of the Plaza de Mayo, they have participated in the search for their missing siblings, most notably the one that led to Victoria Donda and the return of her true identity.

**Kirchner, Néstor** Member of the Peronist Justicialist Party and president of Argentina from 2003 until 2007, when his wife, Cristina Fernández de Kirchner, was elected president. Originally from the south of Argentina, Kirchner was elected president in May 2003, after Carlos Menem, who led the vote count, withdrew from a subsequent runoff. He introduced a politics of inclusion, attracting members from a broad spectrum of political forces into his government. His determination in the fight for human rights made him highly popular. Under his mandate, the laws of Due Obedience and Final Stop, known as the laws of impunity, were abrogated.

**Menem, Carlos** Peronist and second president elected after the return of democracy. Served two successive terms (1989–1995, 1995–1999), modifying the Constitution in 1994 to allow his reelection. He applied the neoliberal policies promoted by the international monetary community, which led to the privatization of the major national industries. In 1990 and 1991, he pardoned the central figures responsible for crimes committed under the last dictatorship and the Montonero leaders who had been imprisoned under the government of Raúl Alfonsín.

**Montoneros** Guerrilla organization that pursued armed struggle between 1970 and 1979, although its roots go back to 1960, during the resistance to the government of President Juan Carlos Onganía. Although they emerged from Peronism, the Montoneros gradually came under the influence of the Movimiento de Sacerdotes para el Tercer Mundo (Movement of Priests for the Third World) and the Cuban Revolution. In

1973, they joined forces with the Fuerzas Armadas Revolucionarias (Revolutionary Armed Forces, or FAR), a move that consolidated their revolutionary Marxist politics. After the return of Juan Domingo Perón to Argentina, the irreconcilable differences between the Montoneros, the unions, and the Peronist right led to a break, and the Montoneros went underground. Following their violent suppression under the last dictatorship, fractured by dissent among their leaders, the Montoneros finally disappeared in 1979. Their main leaders were Juan Manuel Abal Medina (who died in 1972), Norma Arrostito (who disappeared in the ESMA), Mario Firmenich, Roberto Perdía, Fernando Vaca Narvaja, and Rodolfo Galimberti.

**Mothers of the Plaza de Mayo**   On April 30, 1977, a group of mothers with missing sons and daughters demonstrated for the first time before the seat of government on the Plaza de Mayo. From that time on, wearing white scarves on their heads, they gathered every Thursday to demand that those responsible for the crimes committed under the dictatorship be brought to justice and that they be told the whereabouts of their children. Azucena Villaflor, their founder and main leader, was abducted and disappeared in 1978. Today, the Mothers of the Plaza de Mayo have split into two: the founding line continues to fight for the bringing of military criminals to trial, while the association works more to perpetuate the ideals of their disappeared children.

**Proceso de Reorganización Nacional (Process of National Reorganization)**   The name used by the military junta that took power from 1976 to 1983, whose goal was the systematic elimination of those they called the "enemies of the father-land." Thirty thousand people, the majority of them young, were abducted, tortured, and disappeared, and some five hundred children born in captivity or jailed with their parents were "stolen" and placed with families sympathetic to the regime.

**Tumini, Humberto** Founded the Corriente Patria Libre (Free Nation Current) in 1987. Tumini, like so many thousands of other political activists, was imprisoned by the military junta. He was not set free until the return of democracy in 1983. Cofounder of the movement Libres del Sur (Free People of the South), he created a committee to support the candidacy of Néstor Kirchner as president of Argentina and has since held various posts with the governments of both Néstor and Cristina Kirchner.

ALBERTO MANGUEL was born in Buenos Aires and settled in France. He is a member of the Writers' Union of Canada, PEN, and a fellow of the Guggenheim Foundation, and has been named an Officer of the French Order of Arts and Letters. He holds honorary doctorates from the University of Liège in Belgium and the Anglia Ruskin University in Cambridge, England. He has been the recipient of numerous prizes including the Prix Médicis essay prize (France) for *A History of Reading*, the McKitterick Prize (United Kingdom) for his novel *News from a Foreign Country Came*, and the Grinzane Cavour Prize (Italy) for *A Reading Diary*. He also won the Germán Sánchez Ruipérez Prize (Spain) and the Prix Roger Caillois (France) for the ensemble of his work, which has been translated into more than thirty languages.

PABLO A. POZZI is a professor in the history department of the University of Buenos Aires, Argentina, where he specializes in contemporary social history of Argentina and the United States and heads the Oral History Program. He is also on the advisory board to the National Memory Archive in Argentina and is the president of the Argentine Oral History Association (AHORA). He has published a number of books and articles on Argentina and the United States, including *Huellas imperiales. Estados Unidos de la crisis de acumulación a la globalización capitalista* (The United States between crisis and globalization) and *Los setentistas, Izquierda y clase obrera, 1969–1976* (People of the seventies: Culture and life histories of the Argentine left, 1969–1976).